# COTTON, CLIMATE, AND CAMELS
# IN EARLY ISLAMIC IRAN
*A Moment in World History*

Richard W. Bulliet

COLUMBIA UNIVERSITY PRESS

NEW YORK

COLUMBIA UNIVERSITY PRESS

*Publishers Since 1893*

New York    Chichester, West Sussex

Copyright © 2009 Columbia University Press

All rights reserved

Library of Congress Cataloging-in-Publication Data

Bulliet, Richard W.

Cotton, climate, and camels in early Islamic Iran : a moment in world history /

Richard W. Bulliet.

p. cm.

Includes bibliographical references and index.

ISBN 978-0-231-14836-8 (cloth : alk. paper)—ISBN 978-0-231-51987-8 (ebook)

1. Cotton trade—Iran—History.    2. Agriculture—Economic

aspects—Iran—History.    3. Iran—Commerce—History.    4. Iran—History.    I. Title.

HD9086.I72B85 2009

955'.026—dc22    2009007513

Columbia University Press books are printed on permanent and durable acid-free paper.

This book is printed on paper with recycled content.

Printed in the United States of America

c   10 9 8 7 6 5 4 3 2 1

References to Internet Web sites (URLs) were accurate at the time of writing. Neither the
author nor Columbia University Press is responsible for URLs that may have expired or changed
since the manuscript was prepared.

# Contents

# Preface

BEING INVITED TO GIVE the Yarshater Lectures at Harvard University was a double pleasure. First, I have known Professor Ehsan Yarshater as a colleague on the Columbia University faculty for more than thirty years, and I welcomed the opportunity to acknowledge his extraordinary contributions to the field of Iranian studies, particularly such immensely valuable projects as *The Encyclopedia Iranica* and the translation into English of Muhammad b. Jarir al-Tabari's *Ta'rikh al-Rusul wa'l Muluk*. Second, having spent fourteen years at Harvard as student and junior faculty, I enjoyed returning to a place where I had passed many happy years. That my old friend Professor Roy Mottahedeh was the person who extended the speaking invitation and showed unstinting hospitality during the week of the lectures simply compounded this pleasure.

Having delivered the lectures, however, I experienced some uneasiness as I reflected on the conclusion some readers might reach that in elaborating new interpretations of Iranian economic history I had committed myself to a deterministic approach to history. Historians and social scientists have engaged in spirited debates over individual agency in human affairs for some two centuries. Class struggle, environmental conditions, technological capacities, and economic pressures are only a few of the factors that have been put forward as abstract determinants of historical change. Yet every venture into the realm of determinism has been met by vigorous reaffirmations of the principle that human will and human choice, not mechanistic forces, are the dominant factors in history.

Oddly, the field of Middle Eastern history in the pre-modern period has participated little in these debates over agency. It is not that scholars of the Middle East ascribe greater impact to the individual careers of conquerors, rulers, legists, theologians, and mystics than do historians of other parts of the world. It is, rather, that alternative explanations of historical change based on considerations of class, economics, geography, and climate have seldom been raised or widely discussed. To be sure, Leone Caetani once made a case for climatic change as the motor behind the Arab conquests of the seventh/first century,[1] and Eliyahu Ashtor maintained that Egyptian Mamluks were addicted to alcohol because of their cold-weather upbringing in Central Asia and consequently suffered from a sexual impotence that prevented them from reproducing their class.[2] But these and various other deterministic scenarios have generally been shrugged off, both because of flimsiness of evidence and because of a preference for ascribing significant change to the workings of the mind and the spirit, or the power of the sword and the cannon.

Marshall G. S. Hodgson spoke for the majority of historians of medieval Islam when he outlined a "guiding principle" of the work that eventuated in his monumental *The Venture of Islam*:

We may characterize three sorts of individual acts. First, some are historically accidental. . . . Then some are historically cumulative—because they answer to group interests, economic, aesthetic, or even spiritual. . . . But finally, some must be called historically creative. . . . Accidental acts may be decisive in the short run . . . but can generally be disregarded over the long run of history. . . . [For cumulative acts] we must indeed study the play of interests down to the last cynical observation. . . . What I have called creative acts, those that take effect less by being reinforced by other acts in the same interest than by opening up new possibilities to which other persons respond positively, are to be set off for their long-term moral significance.[3]

The common denominator here is the individual act, but in the aggregate—this is what I understand by Hodgson's phrase "historically cumulative"—individual acts commonly result from the play of interests. That is, Hodgson conceives here of people acting as members of groups, and of groups being coerced by pressures from their economic, or even aesthetic and spiritual, environments. In characterizing as "cynical" the observations of historians who study this play of coercive pressures, Hodgson makes clear his disdain for studies that focus on matters over which individuals have no control and concerning which they may not even have active knowledge.

Hodgson contrasts with this the "creative" individual acts that have long-term historical consequences. There is a resemblance between this formulation and Georg Friedrich Hegel's idea of the "world-historical" individual whose actions propel the advances of a Spirit whose progressive realization is the essence and direction of world history. But Hodgson's "creative" individual is assessed according to his long-term moral significance, whereas Hegel absolves his "world-historical" individuals of any normal calculus of moral worth.

What the absolute aim of Spirit requires and accomplishes—what Providence does—transcends the obligations, and the liability to imputation and the ascription of good or bad motives, which attach to individuality in virtue of its social relations. They who on moral grounds, and consequently with noble intention, have resisted that which the advance of the Spiritual Idea makes necessary, stand higher in moral worth than those whose crimes have been turned into the means—under the direction of a superior principle—of realizing the purposes of that principle.[4]

Hodgson distances himself from Hegel by excluding brute conquerors from his category of "creative" historical individuals. His preference is for figures of moral weight, like al-Hallaj or Ibn Taimiya; and in that preference I hear the echo of H. A. R. Gibb's voice lecturing at Harvard in 1960 on what he described as essentially the moral failure of the Umayyad dynasty in the eighth/second century and, by contrast, the fundamentally moral achievement of Saladin in uniting the Muslims against the Crusaders four centuries later.

Moral heroes sometimes overlap Hegel's "world-historical" individuals, Muhammad himself presenting a striking example of this, as Thomas Carlyle famously pointed out in *On Heroes, Hero-Worship, and the Heroic in History* (1840).[5] But my personal affections as a historian have not been for heroes, but for ordinary men and women. I do not consider it cynical to look at the lives of people who had to make hard choices in deciding whether to identify themselves as Muslims or as non-Muslims in the centuries following the Arab conquests, and balanced a variety of social and economic pressures in making those choices. People who elected to become Muslims after lengthy moral or spiritual deliberation in the long run exercised no greater historical agency than those who joined the new religion to gain economic advantage or to please their kinfolk. In the aggregate, they all became indistinguishable in the gradual coming into being of a mass Muslim society. The estimable theologian or mystic whose great-grandfather converted to Islam because he could better support his family by growing cotton for an Arab landlord than by harvesting wheat for a Zoroastrian village chief suffered no moral obloquy because of his materialistic ancestry.

Looking more at the Hegelian notion of individual historical agency, I believe that the decision to seek new grazing grounds made by individual heads of nomadic families facing deteriorating environmental circumstances had a greater impact on history than a tribal khan's dispatch of any number of warrior raiding parties. Raiding parties came and went, and their commanders gained fame for their power and wanton destructiveness; but a folk migration resulting from the aggregate decisions about livestock made by ordinary people outlived the sack of many a great city.

Therefore, in presenting in these lectures a reconstruction of certain Iranian agricultural and climatic developments, and proposing that these developments deeply affected the course of Iranian, and indeed of world, history, I do not see myself as an advocate of economic or climatic determinism. I remain firmly convinced of the importance of individual human agency in history. But I remain equally convinced that decisions taken by ordinary individuals caught up in the complexities and cross-cutting pressures of their personal lives provide a motive force in history that deserves as much recognition and study as the thoughts and deeds of Hodgson's moral heroes or Hegel's "world historical" individuals.

I wish to acknowledge the valuable assistance or advice of several individuals: Ann Kahn and David Koenig, who many years ago collected materials on the weather in Baghdad; Peter Sinnott, who lent me his vast expertise on the geography of Central Asia; Jamsheed Choksy, who did the same on Zoroastrian matters; Asef Kholdani, who guided me in understanding the *Ta'rikh-e Qum*; and Mohsen Ashtiany, who gave me access to the new translation of Bayhaqi that he and C.E. Bosworth were preparing under the sponsorship of Ehsan Yarshater, and who made many invaluable comments on the manuscript; Ramzi Rouighi, whose critical eye for conceptual hyperbole kept me from going overboard farther than I have; and most important, Hossein Kamaly, whose bibliographical expertise, linguistic skills, and appetite for countless hours discussing issues both broad and nit-picking were of untold value. Rosanne D'Arrigo and Gordon Jacoby of the Tree-Ring Laboratory of Columbia's Lamont-Doherty Earth Observatory generously provided invaluable technical assistance. Needless to add, the errors herein are mine alone. I would also like to thank Carole Frohlich for her help on illustrations.

COTTON, CLIMATE, AND CAMELS
IN EARLY ISLAMIC IRAN

# Chapter One
## HOW TO IDENTIFY A COTTON BOOM

THOUGH HISTORIANS HAVE NOT IDENTIFIED the Iranian plateau as a region of economic dynamism, urban expansion, or manufacturing for export in the pre-Islamic period, it became the most productive and culturally vigorous region of the Islamic caliphate during the ninth/third and tenth/fourth centuries, only a century and a half after its conquest by Arab armies.[1] The engine that drove this newfound prosperity was a boom in the production of cotton.

In the eleventh/fifth century the cotton boom petered out in northern Iran while the agricultural economy in general suffered severe contraction. At the same time, Turkish nomads for the first time migrated *en masse* into Iran. These developments resulted in long-term economic change and the establishment of a Turkish political dominance that lasted for many centuries. The engine that drove the agricultural decline and triggered the initial Turkish migrations was a pronounced chilling of the Iranian climate that persisted for more than a century.

Such are the major theses of this book. Though the argumentation to support them will concentrate on Iran, their implications are far-reaching. Iran's prosperity, or lack thereof, affected the entire Islamic world, and through its connections with Mediterranean trade to the west and the growth of Muslim societies in India to the east it affected world history. The same is true of the deterioration of Iran's climate. Not only did it set off the fateful first migration into the Middle East of Turkish tribes from the Eurasian steppe, but it also triggered a diaspora of literate, educated Iranians to neighboring lands that thereby became influenced by Iranian religious outlooks and institutions, and by the Persian language. These broader implications will be addressed in the final chapter, but first the substance of the two theses, which have never before been advanced, must be argued in some detail.

If the evidence to back up the proposition that Iran experienced a transformative cotton boom followed by an equally transformative climate change were abundant, clear, and readily accessible, earlier historians would have advanced them. So what will be presented in the following pages will be less a straightforward narrative than a series of arguments based on evidence that may be susceptible of various interpretations.

With respect to the latter thesis, the cooling of Iran's climate, the crucial evidence is clear, but it only recently became available with the publication of tree-ring analyses from western Mongolia. The question in this case, therefore, is not whether scientifically reliable data exist, but whether or to what degree information proper to western Mongolia can be applied to northern Iran over 1500 miles away. This question, along with a variety of corroborative information, will be addressed in chapters 3 and 4.

The case for an early Islamic cotton boom, on the other hand, rests on published sources that have long been available. However, these sources only yield their secrets to quantitative analysis, as will be seen in this chapter and the next. The methodology of applying quantitative analysis to published biographical dictionaries and other textual materials constitutes a third theme of this book.

In 1970, Hayyim J. Cohen published a quantitative study of the economic status and secular occupations of 4200 eminent Muslims, most of them ulama and other men of religion. He limited his investigation to those who died before the year 1078/470.[2] Overall, he surveyed 30,000 brief personal notices in nineteen compilations that are termed in Arabic *tabaqat*, or "classes." These works are generally referred to in English as biographical dictionaries. The subset of notices that he extracted for quantitative analysis were those for whom he found specific economic indicators—to wit, occupational epithets like Shoemaker, Coppersmith, or Tailor—included as part of the biographi-

cal subject's personal name. All the compilations Cohen used covered the
entire caliphate from North Africa to Central Asia. None was devoted to a
specific province or city, except for a multivolume compilation specific to the
Abbasid capital of Baghdad.

Commercial involvement with textiles, Cohen found, was the most common economic activity indicated by occupational epithets, and from this he
inferred that the textile industry was the most important economic mainstay
of the ulama in general. For individuals dying during the ninth/third and
tenth/fourth centuries, textiles accounted for a remarkably consistent 20 to
24 percent of occupational involvement. He does not specify which epithets
he included in the "textiles" category, or the relative importance of each of
them, but the master list of trades that accompanies his article includes producers and sellers of silk, wool, cotton, linen, and felt, along with articles of
clothing made from these materials. (Whether he classed furs with textiles
or with leather goods is unclear.)

Cohen's sample amounted to only 14 percent of the total number of
biographies he surveyed because in an era before surnames became fixed
and heritable, individuals were distinguished by a variety of epithets (e.g.,
place of origin or residence, occupation, official post, distinguished ancestor), some chosen by themselves and some derived from the usage of others.
Nevertheless, it is reasonable to assume that the occupational distribution
of the 14 percent identified by the name of a trade roughly mirrors the economic profile of the entire 30,000. Scholarship on Islamic subjects, by and
large, was not a highly remunerative activity in the Muslim societies prior
to the twelfth/sixth century. So most Muslim scholars, unlike Christian
clergy supported by the revenues of churches or monasteries, had to earn a
secular livelihood to maintain their families. To be sure, the son of a prosperous trader or craftsman who had the leisure to become highly educated
in religious matters might have taken the occupational name of his father
without himself engaging in the trade indicated, but it seems unlikely that
he would have adopted an occupational name entirely unrelated to his or his
family's position in the economy. Whether at first or second hand, then, the
abundance of textile-related names, as opposed to the total absence of, say,
Fishers or Potters, almost certainly reflects the broad economic reality of
the class of people included in the biographical dictionaries.

Cohen's study provides a baseline against which to compare a parallel analysis of a large biographical compilation devoted to a single city, the metropolis of Nishapur in the northeastern Iranian province of Khurasan.[3] With a population that grew from an estimated 3000 to nearly 200,000 during the period of Cohen's survey, Nishapur was one of the most dynamic and populous cities in the caliphate, probably ranking second only to Baghdad itself.[4] Compiled in many volumes by an eminent religious scholar known as al-Hakim al-Naisaburi, this work survives today only in an epitome that contains little information beyond the names of its biographical subjects. But that is sufficient for our purposes.

Table 1.1 shows that in each of the periods covered, the proportion of individuals engaged in basic textile trades in Nishapur ("Total Textiles") is 50 to 100 percent higher than the proportions uncovered by Cohen for the caliphate in general. The dominant role of textiles in the economic lives of Nishapur's religious elite would have loomed still larger if tailors and vendors of specific types of garments had been included, but they have been left out, since it is uncertain which of them may have been included in Cohen's calculations.

TABLE 1.1    Occupational epithets in al-Hakim's *Ta'rikh Naisabur*

| DATES CE/AH | PERIOD 1:<br>795–863/179–249 | PERIOD 2:<br>863–906/249–293 | PERIOD 3:<br>906–926/293–314 | PERIOD 4:<br>926–994/314–384 |
|---|---|---|---|---|
| QATTAN:<br>Cotton farmer | 0 | 4 | 5 | 8 |
| BAZZAZ:<br>Cotton cloth<br>dealer | 3 | 6 | 7 | 10 |
| KARABISI:<br>Dealer in heavy<br>duty cotton<br>cloth | 0 | 1 | 3 | 15 |
| COTTON TOTAL | 3 (11%) | 11 (22%) | 15 (35%) | 33 (42%) |
| OTHER TEXTILE<br>TRADES | 8 | 8 | 0 | 7 |
| TOTAL<br>TEXTILES | 11 (40%) | 19 (38%) | 15 (35%) | 40 (51%) |
| TOTAL<br>ALL TRADES | 27 | 50 | 46 | 78 |

Looking specifically at the tenth/fourth century, cotton growers and cotton fabric vendors alone accounted for 35 to 42 percent of all occupational epithets in Nishapur. This elevated level was noted by Cohen: "As for cotton, the biographies of Muslim religious scholars indicate that Khurasan province was a big centre for its manufacture."[5] This preponderance of cotton farmers and merchants is all the more striking in view of the absence on the table of any cotton growers at all down to the final third of the ninth/third century. In other words, if Iran really did experience a transformative cotton boom, as is being argued here, it would seem to have reached Nishapur only in the late ninth/third century. As we shall see later, however, other types of data show that cotton began to become a major enterprise farther to the west, in central Iran, a century earlier.

Also of interest is the fact that during Period 1 of table 1.1, which immediately preceded the apparent start of the boom in Nishapur, five of the people dealing in textiles other than cotton traded in felt, a commodity produced mainly by nomads in Central Asia and imported into Iran by caravan. This hint that Central Asian imports still dominated Nishapur's fiber market in the early ninth/third century is reinforced by the fact that there are also five fur merchants recorded for the period. (Since I am not certain whether Cohen considered fur a textile, I have not included furriers in the table.) In sum, felt and fur, two products coming from beyond Iran's northeastern frontier, together made up 30 percent of all textile/fiber commerce conducted by Nishapur's religious elite before the rise of cotton.

The occupational preferences of Nishapur's ulama apparently changed from imported felts and furs to locally produced cotton. The data from Period 3 covering the last third of the ninth/third century, 863 to 906/250–315, confirm this shift. Cotton was then clearly emerging as a major new product, going from 11 percent to 22 percent of all trade epithets, but three felt merchants and two furriers are still recorded for this period. However, during Periods 3 and 4, covering the period down to the start of the eleventh/fifth century, felt dealers disappear from al-Hakim's compilation, with only one furrier mentioned. Imported fibers were no longer of major interest to Nishapur's religious elite.

For the skeptically inclined reader, deducing a cotton boom from the changing percentages of occupational names distributed among a couple of hundred religious scholars may seem strained. But leaving precise numerical calculations aside, cotton clearly became an important part of the Iranian economy during the early Islamic centuries. The comparison with Cohen's data indicates a role for cotton in Iran that was far greater than that played by all textile production combined in the caliphate as a whole, particularly considering that if he had chosen to systematically exclude Iranians from his tabulations, his total for non-Iranian ulama involvement in textile trading would have been appreciably lower.

An even more striking attestation to the historical significance of cotton's emergence as a key product in the Iranian agricultural economy, however, is the fact that little or no cotton seems to have been grown on the Iranian plateau during the Sasanid period prior to the Arab conquests of the seventh/first century.[6] The soundness of this statement is fundamental to the argument of this chapter. Hence, the evidence on which it is based needs to be explored in some detail.

Although at least one scholar, Patricia L. Baker in her book *Islamic Textiles*, has asserted that large quantities of cotton were exported from eastern Iran to China before the rise of Islam,[7] *The Cambridge History of Iran* takes a more cautious position: "The study of Sasanian textiles . . . is hampered by an almost total lack of factual information. The meagerness of the historical sources is matched by the paucity of textile documents."[8] The discussion that follows this introductory sentence deals extensively with silk and secondarily with wool. Cotton is nowhere mentioned.

Nevertheless, Baker's statement refers to trade with China and to "eastern Iranian" provinces that may have been outside the borders of the Sasanid empire. In fact, evidence from east of the Sasanid frontier, which roughly coincided with the current frontier between Iran and Turkmenistan, does confirm the presence of cotton cultivation there, but it falls well short of indicating large-scale production or trade. Moreover, it strongly implies links with India rather than with the Sasanid-ruled Iranian plateau.[9]

Archaeologists have dated some cottonseeds excavated in the agricultural district of Marv, northeast of today's Iranian border, to the fifth century CE, and cotton textiles have been found in first-century CE royal burials of the Kushan dynasty in northern Afghanistan.[10] At the other end of the Silk Road, there are occasional Chinese textual references to cotton "from the Han dynasty [ended 220 CE] or later,"[11] and in 331 CE an embassy from the

Central Asian principality of Ferghana, today part of Uzbekistan, arrived at a royal court in Gansu in northwest China with tribute goods that included cotton and coral.

The mention of coral is a first clue that India played a key role in the spread of cotton to Central Asia. India was not only the land of origin of cultivated cotton but also a much more likely source of coral than Iran. Moreover, the Kushan and post-Kushan periods (i.e., the first five centuries CE) saw a prodigious territorial expansion of Indian Buddhism in western Central Asia, providing the basis for the entry of Buddhism into China. The names are recorded of some 150 Buddhist pilgrims, both Indian and Chinese, who passed through Gansu, the province linking northern China with Inner Asia, and helped spread Buddhism in China between the second and sixth centuries.[12] Surviving itineraries of these wayfarers demonstrate that the normal practice for pilgrims seeking sacred manuscripts in India was to travel northwestward through Gansu, then traverse the Silk Road to Sogdia (today Uzbekistan), a region of non-Sasanid Iranian-speaking principalities east and north of the Oxus River; and finally, to turn southward to Bactria, the old Kushan territory in northern Afghanistan. From there they traversed the high passes of the Hindu Kush Mountains before descending into India. Though many stops at Buddhist monasteries en route are detailed in the written accounts, none indicates an extension of the pilgrim journey into Sasanid Iran. With respect to the relative importance of cotton as a trade good along this route, recent Chinese excavations at Khotan, a major entrepot on the Silk Road, have unearthed many textile fragments, 85 percent of them wool, 10 percent silk, and only 5 percent cotton.[13] Other sources stress the predominance of silk as a trade good.[14]

Philology also points to India as the point of origin of the cotton reaching China from Bactria and Sogdia. The word for *cotton* in the Iranian language spoken at Khotan, known as Khotanese Saka, was *kapaysa*, a word that later appears as *kaybaz* in the eastern Turkic languages of Inner Asia. The word is clearly derived from Sanskrit *karpasa*, meaning *cotton*. Of similar derivation is the Persian word *karbas*, which in later Muslim times designated a kind of heavy cotton cloth.[15]

The occupational name Karabisi, which appears in table 1.1, that became frequent in Nishapur toward the end of the tenth century literally means "a dealer in *karabis*," the plural of *karbas*. The form of this plural, however, is Arabic, not Persian, which would normally be *karbas-ha*. Because Arabic was heard only rarely in northeastern Iran prior to the fall of the Sasanid empire to invading Arab armies, the implication is that even though Sanskrit-derived words for cotton were known in Central and Inner Asia before the advent of Islam, the term *karbas* only entered Khurasan during the Islamic period. This would also accord with the comparatively late popularity of the word *karbas* in the Nishapur cotton industry. *Karabisi* is very uncommon as an occupational name farther west in Iran, where cotton came to be cultivated earlier than in Nishapur.

To sum up, before the Arab conquest cotton was grown, but was of limited commercial importance, in the vicinity of Central Asian urban centers such as Marv, Bukhara, Samarqand, and Ferghana, all of which had river water available for irrigation during the summer growing season. Although it is impossible to prove that its cultivation was unknown on the Iranian plateau,[16] it was only after the Arab conquest that cotton took off as a major commercial crop in central Iran, which was almost entirely lacking in river water during the long, hot summers it needed to grow. This poses several crucial questions: Who introduced cotton to the Iranian plateau? Where was it grown? How was it irrigated? To whom was it sold? Why was it so successful? And, most enigmatically, what was its connection to the Islamic religion?

Before addressing these questions, we must start with some background. Historians generally recognize that the early Islamic centuries witnessed a remarkable surge of urbanization and cultural production in the piedmont areas surrounding the deserts of the central Iranian plateau. Cities like Nishapur, Rayy, and Isfahan, which had not previously ranked as major urban centers, grew to accommodate populations of more than 100,000 souls. Historians who have taken note of this growth have advanced several causative explanations, from Andrew Watson's hypothesis that the spread of new crops increased calorie production and thereby touched off a demographic surge,[17] to my own suggestion that conversion to Islam triggered a migration from countryside to city,[18] to a more diffuse effort to relate the Muslim political unification of lands previously ruled by the Byzantine and Sasanid emperors to overall economic growth. What all of these approaches lack, to a greater or lesser degree, is a foundation in Iranian economic data.

The economic history of medieval Islam is a notoriously intractable subject. Financial documents of even the most rudimentary sort are virtually nonexistent, and economic matters rarely arise in the more discursive writings of the period. To be sure, coinage is abundant and carries informative inscriptions, but only spotty information is available about the relationship of the gold dinars and silver dirhams studied by numismatists to actual commercial transactions: What did things cost? What were people paid? What was the volume of production?[19]

Geographers and travelers do touch now and again on such relevant matters as trade routes, export commodities, and manufactures. But their comments seldom enlighten us on matters of quantity, value, and personnel engaged. We learn, for example, that rhubarb, turquoise, and edible clay were all prized exports from Nishapur, but we don't know whether the annual volume of these goods was measured in tens of pounds or in thousands of pounds, much less how much a typical shipment might be worth, who its buyers were, or how many people were engaged in its production and shipping.

Textiles, of course, are different from rarities or luxuries like rhubarb and turquoise. They have long played a disproportionate part in world trade. People everywhere need to clothe themselves, and it is not unusual for imported fibers, as opposed to those that are locally produced, to dominate a region's textile markets. Chinese silk in late antiquity; Spanish and English wool in late medieval and early modern Europe; American, Egyptian, and Indian cotton in the nineteenth century; and Australian wool in the twentieth century afford outstanding examples of fibers playing a powerful role in export economies.

Prior to modern times, no export product could achieve market dominance unless it commanded a market of sufficient size and profitability to offset the costs and risks of land or sea transportation, which were unfailingly expensive, perilous, and slow. For long-distance trade, the most desirable commodities were light in weight, high in value, steady in demand, easily packaged, and unaffected by slowness of transport. Fresh foods that could spoil or suffer from rough handling did not travel far, but dried or preserved foodstuffs did. At different times and places, vegetable oils; wine; grains; dried beans, fruits, and nuts; and salted fish, pork, or beef have all fed lucrative export markets. Nevertheless, some of these commodities were of such low unit value that high volumes were necessary to turn a good profit. By contrast, products that fit into the luxury category, such as spices, aromatics, dyestuffs, and gemstones, tended to be low in bulk and high in profit. However, demand for these items was often variable, because there is a limit to the amount of myrrh, ginger, or emeralds a society can absorb. In addition, some of these products, such as nutmeg, high-quality frankincense, and lapis lazuli, came from narrowly restricted locales, in the cases cited, Indonesia's Banda Islands, Oman's Dhufar province, and Afghanistan's Badakhshan region.

Unlike all the previously mentioned products, textile fibers meet every test of market suitability. Whether shipped raw, as thread or yarn, or as finished fabric, textile fibers resist spoilage, pack efficiently, enjoy steady demand, and, depending on the degree of processing and fabrication, can have monetary values that are comparatively high in relation to bulk. Among these fibers, animal hair (used to make felt) and wool adapt less easily to changing demand than do cotton, flax, or silkworm filament. To be sure, Spain and England in their time witnessed deliberate large-scale conversions of cropland into pasturage in order to increase the production of wool. However, considerably less flexibility existed in regions like the Middle East, where animal husbandry took the form of wide-ranging nomadism in arid or semiarid regions. The nomads themselves fabricated woolen goods and felts for their own use and for occasional sale, but most grazing took place too far from a commercial center to make large-scale marketing of fleeces or hair convenient. A marketer interested in meeting or stimulating increased consumer demand would have had to improve collecting and marketing techniques, or enlarge the area devoted to pasture, or both. Because the producers were so often on the move, the former option was difficult. And so was the latter, because it was likely to involve conflicts with cultivators or landowners who had vested interests in keeping animals off their sown fields. So fiber production has usually played a secondary role in the pastoral nomadic economies of the Middle East and Central Asia. Trans-Asian camel caravans, for example, once included men with large sacks who trailed after the two-humped camels as they molted in the springtime and collected for eventual sale the camel hair that fell off or snagged on bushes. But this was purely ancillary to the camels' main use as beasts of burden.

With vegetable fibers and the mulberry leaves that nurture silk worms there is inherently greater flexibility. As with most other agricultural crops, the acreage under production can increase or decrease, depending on market conditions. Yet cotton, linen, and silk differ substantially in their technical requirements.[20] The case of silk, where silkworms have to be nurtured and then killed and the fiber of their cocoons painstakingly unwound, is well known. But linen production too entails great labor. After the flax seeds are removed by combing, the plant's inner fibers must be freed. This process, known as retting, involves either partial decomposition in the field or the application of great amounts of running water. Then comes a drying stage, which is followed by braking, scutching, and hacking processes in which the fibers are freed from the boon, or woody portion of the plant. Once these steps have been completed, the fiber that remains for spinning amounts to only 15 percent of the harvested flax plant.

In comparison, cotton processing is less complicated and less onerous. The primary operations include beating the bolls to separate the fibers and remove any clinging bits of soil, removing the seeds by hand or with a gin, and carding, which consisted of raking the fibers out for spinning.[21] In addition, cotton enjoys another advantage over flax and silk as an export commodity. The flax plant and mulberry tree can grow in a wide range of temperate climates, but cotton is strictly a warm-weather plant. Thus whenever cotton cloth has become known and its qualities appreciated in a temperate region that does not have the long, hot growing season and abundant water needed for local cultivation, a demand for imported fabrics has usually followed.

It may be hyperbolic to conclude from these considerations that cotton is historically the most important product ever in interregional trade, but the capacity of cotton farming to support entire economies is beyond question. The histories of India, the Nile Valley, the American South, and Soviet Central Asia all testify to this. The question to be asked with respect to Iran, therefore, is not whether cotton cultivation had the potential to transform the medieval Iranian economy, but whether in fact it did so.

Evidence on economic matters is as woefully lacking for the pre-Islamic period of Iranian history as it is for the early Islamic period. Studies of Sasanid
Iran usually speak only in generalities about agriculture on the Iranian plateau. Scholars concur that the primary crops were wheat and barley and that
various other foodstuffs were produced in smaller quantities for local consumption. In the area of agricultural technology, scholars are reasonably certain that the most distinctive feature of Iranian farming, the use of underground canals known as qanats to bring irrigation water to thirsty fields,
dates as far back as the Achaemenid period of the sixth to fourth centuries
BCE.[22] Nevertheless, there is no measure of how frequently crops were irrigated by qanat, as opposed to springs and artesian wells, natural precipitation, seasonal runoff, or surface streams and canals.

Within the general profile of the agricultural economy of the Sasanid
Empire, Iran's plateau region seems to have produced only a few exportable
commodities, mostly nuts, dried fruits, and saffron. Control of the land lay
in the hands of great lords and lesser gentry, who are usually described as enjoying a rural lifestyle. The model of manorial life familiar from descriptions
of the agricultural economy of medieval Europe, with, in the Iranian case, a
lord's adobe brick castle and outbuildings and one or more nearby villages
forming a self-sufficient economic unit, is perhaps not too farfetched. Villagers were more or less self-sufficient after the lord had taken his share of
the harvest. Wheat and barley provided basic sustenance for man and beast.
When taxes were collected in kind, substantial quantities of grain might be
laid up in government storehouses, but there is little reason to suppose that
grain was ever exported in significant quantity from the plateau region. There
were no seaports or navigable rivers, and overland transport was too expensive for such bulky and low-value commodities. Instead, the stored grain was
probably allocated, as it would later be under Muslim rule, to local military
and administrative personnel, to armies in transit, or occasionally to the al-
leviation of hardship caused by drought or other local catastrophes.

Cities on the Iranian plateau, particularly in the north along the western
portion of the Silk Road running from today's Turkmenistan frontier to the

Baghdad region in Iraq, seem typically to have been composed of a garrisoned fortress adjoining a walled enclosure. Judging from standard ratios of medieval urban density, the total walled area of such a city could typically accommodate a few thousand people. However, the existence of open space within the walls for sheltering villagers during times of rural unrest favors the lower end of these population estimates, around 3000 to 5000 people. In addition to providing local security against marauders, the purpose of these cities was primarily servicing and protecting the caravan trade between Mesopotamia and Central Asia, China, or India. In the southwest, the provinces of Fars and Khuzistan seem to have had somewhat larger urban centers and to have been more strongly linked to the comparatively well-urbanized culture of Mesopotamia.

Information about fiber use in the Sasanid period relates mostly to the elite strata of society. Visual evidence, surviving fabric specimens, and textual references show clearly that the upper classes favored silk garments woven with elaborate patterns. Vegetable and animal motifs within repeating geometric settings are commonly represented (fig. 1.1). Though Iranians eventually became abundant producers of silk, much Sasanid silk came from China as a staple of Silk Road caravans.[23] Many patterns, however, were distinctly Iranian, indicating either that imported silk thread was woven into fabric after it reached Iran or that Chinese exporters designed fabrics specifically for export. The weaving techniques used in Sasanid fabrics were quite sophisticated, but little is known of weaving as a trade. If weaving in the Islamic period followed earlier occupational patterns, it is likely that weavers did not enjoy high social status in Sasanid Iran. As for ordinary villagers, little is recorded about their garments, though wool was undoubtedly in use, possibly alongside linen or hemp.

The accepted grand narratives of Iranian history take for granted the role of the plateau region as a rural hinterland for the capital province in lower Mesopotamia. They describe a land dominated by warrior nobles whose lives centered on warfare, hunting, and feasting, and whose aesthetic sense was most fully gratified by silk brocade garments and gold and silver plates and drinking vessels. A vast gulf yawned between these nobles and the common villagers, and there was little in the way of a middle social stratum. In the absence of large and dynamic cities, manufacturing and marketing were poorly developed.

FIGURE 1.1. Example of Sasanid silk brocade. (By permission of the Metropolitan Museum of Art.)

In the early Islamic centuries this pattern changed. The Arab conquests smashed the power of the Sasanid royal family and diminished (but did not destroy) the domination of the grand baronial families.[24] Though crown estates and firetemple lands became the property of the caliphal state, great landowners and lesser landowning gentry continued to control most agricultural land, as is indicated by the frequent use of the term *dihqan*, referring to both large and small landowners, in accounts of the period down through the eleventh/fifth century. In the wake of the Sasanid defeat, the Arab victors planted garrisons and governing centers at strategic points throughout the country. These nodes of Muslim Arab influence and control were also economic centers from the very start. Local government officials oversaw the collection of taxes, a sizable portion of which were retained at the governing node, with the rest being sent west to the caliphal capital in Damascus or later Baghdad, or to the holy cities of Mecca and Medina. Of the sums retained locally, a large portion was distributed as military pay to the Arab garrison, which thus acquired purchasing power. Not surprisingly, this new class of warrior consumers attracted artisans and merchants interested in servicing their needs. Many of these were Iranians who converted to Islam and wanted to live in proximity to other Muslims; others were Christians, Jews, or, less frequently, Zoroastrians. Over time these military-administrative nodes of caliphal control grew in size and matured into full-fledged cities. However, this geographical pattern of government and nascent urban development, in and of itself, says nothing about the agricultural hinterland, where Sasanid taxation procedures probably continued with little change during the first century and more of Arab rule.

To make the case for a cotton boom transforming the economy, we will have to explore the linkages between land ownership, irrigation, and the market for agricultural commodities. In schematic form, the remainder of this chapter will argue the following:

1. The new elite of Arab Muslims, along with an initially small number of Iranian converts to Islam, sought to become landowners.

2. In the absence of a policy of displacing the traditional Zoroastrian landowners, the Muslim newcomers utilized a principle of Islamic law that granted ownership to anyone who brought wasteland under production.

3. The vast, arid piedmont areas around Iran's central plateau could be made arable by using the Iranian technological tradition of digging underground irrigation canals (qanats).

4. Qanats were expensive, and the necessity of recruiting farm labor and constructing a village on newly arable desert land added substantially to their cost.

5. Wheat and barley grown on qanat-irrigated land cost more to produce but probably had higher yields than grain irrigated by cheaper means, such as natural rainfall or canals diverting water from surface streams.

6. Unlike wheat and barley, which were normally grown as winter crops, cotton was a summer crop that needed both a long, hot growing season and the steady irrigation that a qanat could supply.

7. As a result of these considerations, wealthy Muslims who wished to become landowners invested in digging qanats and establishing villages on desert lands that they thereby came to own. To make their investments profitable, they planted cotton and fed it into a growing urban textile market, and increasingly into a lucrative export market.

8. For a period of time in the ninth/third century, Iran showed signs of a dual agriculture economy in which traditional Zoroastrian landowners grew primarily winter grains and Muslims grew primarily summer cotton.

Some of these propositions, especially the phrase "dual agricultural economy" in the final point, sound altogether too modern for the period we are dealing with. They assume a degree of market rationality that certainly did not exist. They ignore local social, political, and economic variables, including such obvious matters as proximity to markets. And they imagine a calculus of agricultural investment that is unrealistically isolated from noneconomic factors, such as rural security, ethnic friction, and family rivalries and rankings. They also ignore the fact that in Central Asian areas that already had some familiarity with cotton growing, such as Marv in today's Turkmenistan and Bukhara and Samarqand in today's Uzbekistan, qanats were not used. There crops of every sort were irrigated by canals carrying water from the Murghab and Zeravshan rivers.

Nevertheless, these propositions briefly describe, *grosso modo*, what happened in some of Iran's northern piedmont areas, and they call attention to three issues in particular: the problem of land ownership in a postconquest situation, the connection between investment and irrigation, and the connection between Muslims in particular and the growing of cotton. Just as earlier we used quantifiable evidence from a single Iranian city to illustrate the major role that cotton played in the medieval Iranian economy, as seen from the position of the Muslim religious elite, so the quantifiable evidentiary base for the propositions we have just given will come mostly from a single district centered on the city of Qom, which was largely established by immigrant Arabs and has become, today, Iran's paramount center for religious education. Our argument will center on place-name analysis and tax data.

Place-name analyses have proven of great historical value in virtually every part of the world.[25] Names placed on the land often last for centuries and tell the tale of population movements, political and social change, and linguistic evolution. In Iran, however, village names do not seem to be particularly durable. For example, around Nishapur scarcely a single village name survives from the pre-Mongol period. Although this could be seen as testifying to the destruction of civilized life so often ascribed to the era of Mongol dominion in the thirteenth/seventh century, it may equally stem from the long-term self-destructive nature of qanat irrigation. No matter how carefully an underground canal is engineered and maintained, water running through earth will eventually take its toll. When a qanat eventually caves in, there may be no alternative but to abandon the village it served and pioneer a new qanat and village nearby.

Can qanat-irrigated villages be distinguished by name from other villages? To explore that question with a view to analyzing village names in the early Islamic centuries, we will look at a distinctive class of names for inhabited places (as opposed to rivers, mountains, etc.) that accounts for a large share of all of Iran's toponyms today. This class consists of compounds in which the first element refers to a person, usually by name but sometimes by title, position, or other identifier, and the second element is *abad*, which identifies the place as built and inhabited. For convenience sake I will term this the *fulanabad* pattern, using the Arabic-derived word *fulan*, meaning "somebody" or "so-and-so," as a placeholder for the personal designator that begins the compound.

A plausible supposition is that the person named in the first part of a *fulanabad* compound is the person who "founded" the town or village, though what "founding" consists of is not immediately evident or always the same.

Support for this supposition may be found in India, where the handful of
*fulanabad* place-names (e.g., Heydarabad, Ahmedabad) listed in the index of
*A Historical Atlas of South Asia* are mostly substantial cities that can readily
be identified with a historical founder whose act of foundation is preserved
in the name.[26] In Iran, however, scarcely any sizable cities have *fulanabad*
names. The overwhelming majority of the many thousands of *fulanabads*
are villages. In a small percentage of cases, the name of the village does suggest formal establishment by a ruler or official (e.g., Shah-abad, Soltan-
abad), but the vast preponderance of the *fulan* elements in Iranian village
names cannot be identified with any particular ruler or official. For Iran's
*Ostan-e Markazi*, or "Central Province," which includes both Tehran and
Qom, the top ten *fulanabad* names listed in the *Farhang-i Jughrafiyai-i
Iran*, an exhaustive gazetteer published between 1949 and 1954, are listed in
table 1.2.

This list suggests that if *fulanabad* villages are typically named after their
founders, then the founders of the villages that exist today were mostly neither rulers nor officials, because over the last two centuries or so such illustrious individuals have more often been identified by title or honorific epithet
than by an unadorned given name. This does not resolve the issue of "found-

TABLE 1.2    Modern village names in Ostan-e Markazi

| VILLAGE NAME | NUMBER OF VILLAGES |
| --- | --- |
| Hosein-abad | 44 |
| Ali-abad | 31 |
| Hajji-abad | 23 |
| Hasan-abad | 22 |
| Mohammad-abad | 21 |
| Ahmad-abad | 21 |
| Abbas-abad | 18 |
| Mahmoud-abad | 18 |
| Qasem-abad | 17 |
| Karim-abad | 14 |

*Source:* Farhang-i Jughrafiai-i Iran (Tehran: Dayirah-i
Jughrafiai-i Sitad-i Artish, 1328–1332 [1949–54]), 9 v.

ing," however. The personal name attached to a *fulanabad* village could be that of the owner of the village, rather than the founder. In this case, the *fulan* part of the name might have changed when the village passed from one owner to another. Yet this seems unlikely. Surviving eighteenth-/twelfth- and nineteenth-/thirteenth-century documents recording land sales make it clear that village ownership was commonly divided among several parties.[27] Deeds of sale covering between one and five sixths of a village—each sixth called a *dang*—are as common as those transferring full ownership. Yet the village has only one name, and the deeds do not indicate a change in that name. In addition, it seems unlikely that any tax administration would have tolerated the sort of rapid changes in name that might occur at a time of rural disorder or volatility in the real estate market that might have caused villages to change hands often.

The not infrequent employment of the name form *fulanabad-fulan*, wherein a personal name different from that included in the primary *fulanabad* compound is appended to the compound, may have been a convenient way of indicating current ownership without changing the foundation name of the village. Many of these appended *fulans* contain precisely administrative ranks, honorific titles, or other markers of individual identity that are almost wholly absent from *fulanabad* names proper. (As table 1.3 shows, the word or words following a *fulanabad* name also include terms that are not proper names or personal epithets.)

Proceeding on the assumption that the initial personal components of *fulanabad* names do indeed reflect the names of village "founders," we will ignore these words that come after *fulanabad* and look at the full array of the initial personal components as a reflection of the personal names in use among what we may tentatively term "the village founder class." The names in table 1.2, for example, are all among the most common Iranian male given names of the pre–World War II era. But a list of the most popular names in the ninth/fourth century, the period of our putative cotton boom, would be quite different. Most notably, the third most frequent *fulan*, the title Hajji, or "Mecca Pilgrim," which in post-Mongol times became so important in many parts of the Muslim world as to effectively substitute for a personal name, never appears as a part of a personal name in the biographical dictionaries of the earlier period.

TABLE 1.3    Examples of names and terms suffixed to modern *fulanabad*
village names

| PERSONS | ADMINISTRATIVE STATUS |
|---|---|
|  | Khaleseh |
| Bu al-Ghaisas | Shahi |
| Kadkhoda Hossein | TRIBES |
| Hajji Qaqi | Inanlu |
| Hajji Agha Mohammad | Ahmadlu |
| Arbab Kaikhusro | Afshar |
| HONORIFIC TITLES | Qajar |
| Amir Amjad | PHYSICAL FEATURES |
| Majd al-Dowleh | Olya (upper) |
| Dabir al-Soltan | Sofla (lower) |
| Qavvam al-Dowleh | Wasat (middle) |
| Moshir al-Soltaneh | Kuchek (small) |
| Ain al-Dowleh | Bozorg (large) |

The question of what can be concluded from the personal components of
early *fulanabad* toponyms will arise again later, but other characteristics of
*fulanabad* villages must be explored first. The most important of these is water supply. The 1949–54 gazetteer includes for most villages a note as to their
source or sources of water. Tabulating these sources for the interior piedmont
regions of Iran, it becomes apparent that there is a high correlation between
the *fulanabad* name form and irrigation by qanat. In the *Ostan-e Markazi* 765
out of 2708 villages, or 35 percent, bore a *fulanabad* name. For 133 of these the
gazetteer listed no water source. However, of the remainder, 75 percent—473
out of 632—were watered by qanat. As for villages bearing some other name
form, only 34 percent were watered by qanat. By comparison, in the Caspian
provinces, where rainfall supplies water in abundance, qanats are almost nonexistent; accordingly, *fulanabad* village names rarely occur.

The correlation between a *fulanabad* name and qanat irrigation is far
from absolute; but it is sufficiently striking to raise the suspicion that in the
case of *fulanabad* villages, "founding" a village involved paying for the dig-

ging of a qanat. It must be noted, however, that there is considerable disagreement among Iranian scholars on just this point. On the one hand, Aly Mazaheri, the Iranian scholar who translated into French an Arabic treatise
written in 1017/407 on the calculations entailed in engineering a qanat, remarks in his introduction:

> Having discovered water, studied the terrain, and provided the under-
> ground channel to the fields destined to be irrigated, the "waterlord"
> [*hydronome*: English equivalent patterned on "landlord"] built the vil-
> lage. In Eastern Iran (Khurasan) he bore the prestigious name of payda-
> gar: the discoverer, the midwife, the pioneer, the founder, the creator of
> the village. It is thus that the term apady, "irrigation," has come to mean
> "water source," village, cultivation, town, civilization, and that the word
> abad, "irrigated by," follows the name of the founder in designating so
> many sites of Persian civilization between the Bosphorus and the Gan-
> ges. Thus beside Ali-Abad, Mohammad-Abad, Hossein-Abad, etc., so
> numerous in Iran, we have Hyder-Abad, Ahmad-Abad, Allah-Abad, etc.
> throughout the vast world where Persian was once the administrative
> language.[28]

A contrary view is maintained by the Iranian sociologist Ahmad Ashraf.
Writing in the *Encyclopaedia Iranica*, he defines the word "Abadi" as:

> Persian term meaning "settlement, inhabited space;" it is applied basi-
> cally to the rural environment, but in colloquial usage it often refers to
> towns and cities as well. The Persian word derives from Middle Persian
> apat, "developed, thriving, inhabited, cultivated" (see H. S. Nyberg, *A
> Manual of Pahlavi II,* Wiesbaden, 1974, p. 25); the Middle Persian word
> is based on the Old Iranian directional adverb a, "to, in" and the root pa,
> "protect" (AIR Wb., cols. 300ff, 330, 886). Some Iranian social scientists
> have suggested an analysis into ab "water" and a suffix –ad . . . and this
> error is also found in some early modern dictionaries (e.g., Behar-e ʿajam,
> 1296/1879; Asaf al-logat, Hyderabad, 1327–40/1909–21; Farhang-e Anan-
> deraj, 1303/1924).[29]

Though modern philological research must be respected as providing the last word on the subject, the folk etymology associating the word with *ab*, or "water," should not be disregarded. If the early dictionary compilers cited by Ashraf lent their authority to such a folk etymology, it may be that a simple-minded linguistic association between *abad* and "water" has a long enough tradition in popular use to have made it a significant factor in rural naming despite its being philologically in error. That is to say, 100 years ago or a 1000 years ago, a qanat builder thinking about the name to give to his new village may well have had a linguistically incorrect association with water in mind. In any event, the philological debate over whether village founders felt that water was intrinsically associated with the *fulanabad* place-names they opted for has no bearing on the strong quantitative correlation between qanat irrigation and villages designated by such names.

Visualizing the process by which a qanat-watered village comes into being is essential to our historical argument. In thousands of instances, the cultivation of village lands depends entirely on a qanat. However, there are certainly exceptions. Sometimes other water sources exist, and a qanat simply makes the water supply more abundant and more consistent for all purposes year round. In other cases, water from other sources may suffice for growing winter crops (e.g., wheat and barley), which benefit from the winter being the rainy season in most of Iran, but be insufficient for summer crops (e.g., cotton), which grow throughout the hot, dry season and utilize the regular flow from a qanat.

For simplicity's sake, let us assume that as a prospective village founder, you are not simply improving an existing water supply or changing your mix of crops, but creating a village from nothing in a previously uncultivated stretch of desert. Your first step is to call in a specialist in qanat engineering.[30] His job is to site a "mother well" somewhere on the upslope of a nearby range of mountains or hills (fig. 1.2). The "mother well" establishes the depth of the water table and the rate at which water seeps from the surrounding moist soil into an empty well. Once the "mother well" has clarified these conditions, the specialist calculates the direction and length of an underground channel that will lead water by gravity flow from the "mother well" to a point in the arid countryside where it will ultimately flow forth as a surface stream usable for irrigation, drinking, washing, and so forth. He marks

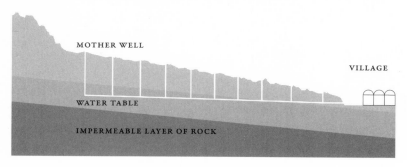

FIGURE 1.2.    Diagram of qanat irrigation tunnel.

that route for the actual diggers and determines the depth of each well to be dug along the qanat's course.

The expertise demanded by these procedures is amply remunerated by the village entrepreneur, for a qanat whose slope is insufficient (i.e., less than approximately 1 meter per thousand) will silt up, and one that is too steep (i.e., more than approximately 3 meters per thousand) will be scoured out and made to collapse by the flow of the water. Because the qanat may extend for several miles beneath ups and downs of hilly terrain, the slope calculation is particularly vital. The eleventh-/fifth-century Arabic treatise on slope calculation mentioned earlier testifies to the skill of the qanat engineer. Written by a noted mathematician, it is one of the few works on practical engineering devoted to agricultural matters in premodern Islamic lands.[31]

Once the qanat engineer has done his job, the village founder brings in experienced qanat diggers to supervise the excavation of the channel. Working backward from the projected point of exit toward the "mother well," the diggers sink wells every 30 meters or so to the depths prescribed by the qanat engineer. When they reach the right depth, a horizontal tunnel is excavated connecting each well with its downstream neighbor. The wells admit air for the diggers and allow the excavated dirt to be hauled up and dumped around the well-head. The dumping creates the characteristic "row of craters" that traces the qanat's course on the surface and, in modern times, is particularly apparent from the air. Candles are used to check the alignment of the tunnel as it grows. The water begins to flow as soon as the tunnel reaches the water table. Only then can the irrigation of the land begin.

Several observations may be made about this scenario. First, there is no presumption that the land on which the village is slated to come into being must be owned by the village founder prior to the digging of the qanat. I am here distinguishing ownership of a specific parcel of land from various broader rights of exploitation that might reside with a monarch, a territorial lord, or a tribe. Rights of the latter sort certainly have existed in Iranian history; but had they normally been asserted so rigidly as to make every newly founded village automatically the property of the monarch, lord, or tribe, it is hard to imagine thousands of individual entrepreneurs investing in the costly and lengthy process of qanat excavation. Nor do narrative sources represent individual rulers or regimes as undertaking the construction of scores or hundreds of qanats. Thus the strong correlation of ordinary male first names with *fulanabad* toponyms, and of the *fulanabad* name pattern with qanat irrigation strongly suggests that individual entrepreneurs did commonly finance qanats. Moreover, surviving documents make it clear that individuals have owned villages and have transferred their ownership by deed of sale for at least several hundred years.

One might draw an analogy between the relationship of a prospective Iranian village founder to a ruler, territorial lord, or tribal leader holding broad territorial rights and the relationship of a homesteader to the U.S. government in the nineteenth century. The federal government owned the nation's undeveloped "public" land categorically, but for a nominal sum it ceded ownership of specific parcels to individual homesteaders on condition that they invest the time and labor needed to make the land productive. The government then benefited from the taxes paid on the product of the land. From at least the late eighth/second century, Islamic law has embodied this reward for entrepreneurship in the form of recognizing freehold ownership for people who make dead land (*ard al-mawat*) productive. The principle was embodied in a *hadith*, or saying of Muhammad, that states: "The rights of ownership belong to him who revives dead land, and no trespasser has any right."[32] However, a famous passage from the second-century BCE Greek historian Polybius relates that the ancient Achaemenid rulers had granted qanat builders five generations of freedom from financial dues, so the exemption in Islamic law may simply have continued a pre-Islamic practice.[33]

A second observation is that the farmers who cultivate the land once the water begins to flow from the qanat cannot be supported by the product of that land from the very outset of the project. Because the land produces nothing and has no inhabitants before the qanat is dug, there can be no stored surpluses from earlier seasons. Thus until the first harvest is brought in, the villagers must gain their sustenance from elsewhere, most likely the resources of the village founder. This obviously makes the investment of the village entrepreneur substantially greater than simply paying for the qanat. He must also supply plow animals, seed, food rations for workers, and building materials for the village houses.

The third observation is that the people who assemble to build a village and cultivate the land in a previously desert locale must come from someplace. How are they assembled? In some modern instances it would appear that prosperous or overpopulated villages sometimes spawned new villages. This process may account for place-names of the *fulanabad-fulan* form that have identical first components but are distinguished only by an adjective in the last element of the name, the adjective in most instances being '*olya* (upper) and *sofla* (lower), or *kuchek* (small) and *bozorg* (large). One might hypothesize that when the earlier of such a pair of villages outgrew its water supply, the landlord decided to dig a new qanat and build a new village nearby using supplies and labor drawn from the original village. But aside from these cases, it seems likely that a person seeking to found a village in a period of static or negative population growth must have borne the burden of recruiting farmers for his entrepreneurial project. Given the hardships that surely would have accompanied the first season or two in a new village, it seems likely that village founders faced with such conditions offered inducements to men who were willing to leave wherever they had been living, possibly against the wishes of their former landlord, and join in the new enterprise.

One form of inducement that seems to have been common was an offer to become part of a *boneh,* or "work team." Unlike landless agricultural laborers or villagers possessing cultivation rights to specific plots of land, members of *bonehs* enjoy a collective right to a share in the produce of village lands.[34] Though the history of the *boneh* system is not well known, it is plausible to imagine a village entrepreneur assembling his initial cohort of cultivators by giving them a stake in the productivity of the village through "work team" membership. This would explain the finding of geographer Javad Safinezhad that the geographical portion of Iran in which the *boneh* system is utilized almost exactly coincides with the area in which qanats are used for irrigation (fig. 1.3).[35] Though Safinezhad makes no specific correlation between *bonehs* and *fulanabad* place-names in particular, it stands to reason that for the modern period that has been the focus of his research, if most *fulanabad* villages had qanats, they also had *bonehs*.

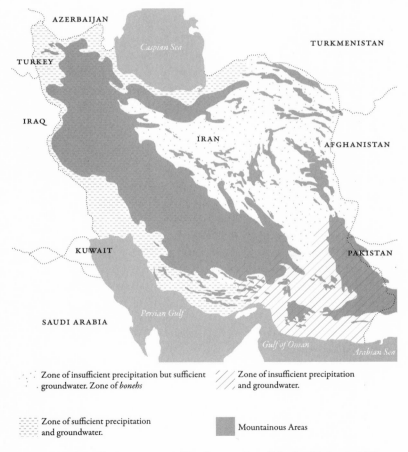

FIGURE 1.3.    Map of water resources and boneh zone in Iran. (After Javad Safinezhad, "The Climate of Iran" ([1977].)

Let me summarize now the tentative conclusions that emerge from this examination of village names from the 1950s:

1. The personal component in *fulanabad* village names probably designates the village "founder," and the idea of "founder" probably includes not only the initial excavation of the village qanat but a variety of other substantial expenses.

2. *Fulanabad* (and probably other) villages were commonly owned by individuals with sufficient freehold rights to permit transfer of the village to another owner by sale.

3. *Fulanabad* names usually do not change when a village changes ownership.

4. The personal components of *fulanabad* names reflect the onomasticon, or name-list, current at the time the villages were founded.

5. *Fulanabad* villages are irrigated by qanat much more often than villages with other sorts of names.

6. Qanat irrigation correlates geographically with the employment of "work teams" (*bonehs*) for cultivating the land.

7. *Fulanabad* villages probably organized their cultivation around *bonehs* more frequently than did non-*fulanabad* villages.

These conclusions are tentative, but they will prove helpful in guiding our efforts to understand the information contained in the earliest large list of village names surviving from the period after the Arab conquest of Iran.

❧

A K. S. Lambton[36] and Andreas Drechsler[37] have written extensively on the early history of the city of Qom and on the contents of *Ta'rikh-e Qom*, a local history compiled in Arabic by Abu Ali Hasan b. Muhammad b. Hasan al-Qummi and translated into Persian in 1402–4/804–6. The Persian translation alone survives, and it contains only five of an original twenty chapters. Hasan al-Qummi began to assemble the work in 963/352 but did not finish it until 990/379 because of a prolonged absence from the city.

Lambton and Drechsler offer many valuable observations relating to the wealth of fascinating information in this work. The protagonists of the his-

torical narrative are Arab settlers of Yemeni tribal background, and the account of their conflicts with the native population, their rise to positions of
dominance in the city of Qom proper, and their arguments with the central
caliphal government over tax assessments is complex, highly detailed, and
minimally related to agricultural production.

However, our current inquiry concerns itself primarily with the information relating to taxation. Lambton notes that Hasan al-Qummi drew on
eight documents that she terms "tax schedules." Drechsler does not entirely
agree with her translation of this unusual Arabic word, *wadi'a*, but for convenience sake I shall follow Lambton's usage. The dates given for the tax schedules encompass the entire ninth/third century:

| | |
|---|---|
| Tax Schedule 1 | 804/188 |
| Tax Schedule 2 | 808/192 |
| Tax Schedule 3 | 836/221 |
| Tax Schedule 4 | 839/224 |
| Tax Schedule 5 | 841/226 |
| Tax Schedule 6 | 897/265 |
| Tax Schedule 7 | 903/290 |
| Tax Schedule 8 | 914/301 |

Although al-Qummi is neither systematic nor complete in his citation of
information from the schedules, it appears that each of them contained inter
alia both the rates of taxation for specific crops and information on individual taxable locales. We shall return later to the matter of tax rates, for our
first concern is with the names of the taxable locales. These are listed in
thirty-four groupings, some labeled *tassuj*, some *rustaq*, and some unlabeled.
Though Lambton states that the term *tassuj* refers to an administrative sub-
district within a larger district called a *rustaq*, a comparison of village names
suggests that in some cases *tassuj* and *rustaq* may have been interchangeable.
For our purposes it is reasonable to proceed on the assumption that all thirty-
four headings given by al-Qummi refer to districts of some sort and the
names listed below them, to taxable locales in those districts.

The task of assembling a definitive list of discrete taxable locales suitable
for comparison with the list of villages so conveniently laid out for the mod-

ern period in the *Farhang-i Joghrafiyai-i Iran* is complicated by al-Qummi's practice of listing in different locations place-names belonging to the same district but coming from different tax schedules. For example, for the district of Tabresh, which may be related to the modern town of Tafresh west of Qom, he lists forty-one taxable locales from Tax Schedule 1; three more from Tax Schedule 3, one of them duplicating a name already given; and thirty-one more from Tax Schedule 5, including sixteen duplicates. In addition to these, Tax Schedule 2 lists thirty-nine names under the rubric Tabresh, none of which overlap the combined fifty-eight names given in the other three schedules. And Tax Schedule 4 lists eight names, which similarly do not duplicate those on the other lists. It would appear, therefore, that there were at least two districts with more or less the same name.

Problems of this sort are compounded by inconsistent spelling and by the absence of any indication of al-Qummi's purpose in listing the names. He does not classify the places listed according to types of ownership or taxation, nor does he indicate why he lists so few names from some districts and so many from others, or why he lists no names at all from Tax Schedules 6 and 7.

After taking into account, to the degree possible, all the duplications and spelling variations, the final composite list totals 1271 names spanning the entirety of the ninth/third century. This would appear to be the longest list of Iranian toponyms specific to a single urban hinterland to survive from the early Islamic period. A comparison of this total with the 2708 villages listed in the 1950s for the entire *Ostan-e Markazi*, the larger region in which Qom is now situated, suggests that al-Qummi's list, despite its peculiarities, probably represents most of the taxable rural locales of his time.

However, one difference between the modern and the medieval lists must be noted. Where 35 percent of the modern names are of the *fulanabad* form, the list from the *Ta'rikh-e Qom* contains only 344 *fulanabad* names, or 26 percent of the total. On the basis of the modern correlation between *fulanabads* and qanat irrigation, one might surmise from this difference that qanat irrigation was not as widely employed in the ninth/third century as in the twentieth/fourteenth. But before exploring this conjecture we should look at the personal names represented in the *fulanabad* compounds (table 1.4).

What stands out in this list of the twelve most common *fulanabad* names is that only one of them, Hormizdabad, is Persian. A look at the complete list

TABLE 1.4.    Fulanabad village names in Ta'rikh-e Qom

| VILLAGE NAME | NUMBER OF VILLAGES WITH NAME |
|---|---|
| Mohammad-abad | 33 |
| Ali-abad | 22 |
| Musa-abad | 11 |
| Yahya-abad | 9 |
| Ahmad-abad | 9 |
| Malik(Milk, Mulk)-abad | 8 |
| Imran-abad | 7 |
| Sulaiman-abad | 7 |
| Hormizd-abad | 7 |
| Hasan-abad | 6 |
| Ishaq-abad | 6 |
| Ja'far-abad | 6 |

of *fulanabads* confirms this low representation of Persian names. At least 80 percent of the *fulanabad* names are clearly Arabic, and the percentage could be a bit higher, because a few names that look Persian might actually be Arabic. This disproportion between Arabic and Persian stands out when we consider village names of the pattern *fulanjird*, in which the second component, *jird* or *gerd*, is often taken to signify the rural estate or manor of one of the gentry. Every one of the twenty-nine *fulanjirds* has a Persian name or word as the first part of the compound.

This comparison puts in relief the dual agricultural economy of early Islamic Iran postulated earlier. If we assume that the association between qanat irrigation and the *fulanabad* name pattern that is apparent in modern toponyms from the Qom region represents a long-standing historical relationship, then it is hard to escape the conclusion that in the ninth/third century, village entrepreneurs who built qanats were overwhelmingly of the Muslim faith, whether they were Arabs or Iranian converts who had taken Arabic names.

Of course, there might be nothing out of the ordinary in this conclusion if it could be established that the central plateau region of Iran had become overwhelmingly Muslim by the early ninth/third century, but this is not the case. In an earlier work entitled *Conversion to Islam in the Medieval Period* I proposed a quantitative technique for estimating the rate of growth of the Muslim community in Iran. In the three decades that have elapsed since that book's publication there have been numerous reservations expressed about the quantitative onomastic method on which it was predicated, but there has been little disagreement with its main finding, namely, that conversion to Islam took place slowly over a period of four centuries or more. In fact, the most challenging criticism, that of Michael Morony, argued that conversion took place at an even slower pace.[38] Thus the once popular "fast calendar" of conversion, which maintained that Islam grew with great rapidity following the Arab conquests, either because of military coercion or from a desire to escape a caliphal head tax (*jizya*) levied on Zoroastrians, Christians, and Jews, has generally been replaced in scholarly circles with a "slow calendar" extending over several centuries (fig. 1.4).

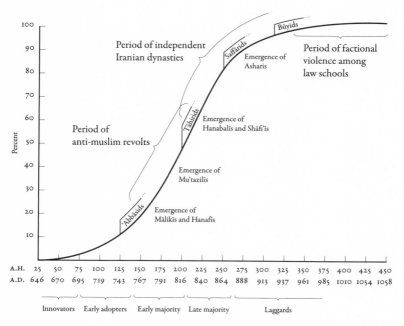

FIGURE 1.4.  Graph of the growth of the Muslim community in Iran. (From Bulliet, *Conversion to Islam* [1979].)

Figure 1.4 reproduces from my earlier book a hypothesized curve of Iranian conversion.[39] It shows that the growth of Iran's Muslim community was approximately 30 percent complete in 804/188, the date of Qom's earliest tax schedule, and 90 percent complete in 914/301, the date of the eighth and last schedule. However, the last schedule made only negligible additions to the list of village names, and no names at all are given from the two schedules preceding it. Thus the effective *terminus ad quem* of the list of village names is the date of Tax Schedule 5, namely, 841/226, by which time the graph of conversion indicates a level of 60 percent.

If, however, as Morony and others have persuasively argued, my onomastic technique underestimates conversion in rural areas, these percentages may be somewhat too high. But they are probably not too low. The consensus view is that Iran in the ninth/third century saw a rapid growth of Islam but was very far from being a predominantly Muslim country until the very end of the century. Even then, large Zoroastrian populations persisted in some rural areas.

The list of most popular *fulanabad* names in table 1.4 provides an additional clue that the villages in question were founded before or toward the beginning of the ninth/third century, when the proportion of Muslims in the population was still quite low, rather than at the end. Four of the twelve names appear in both the Bible and the Quran: Musa = Moses, Yahya = John the Baptist, Sulaiman = Solomon, and Ishaq = Isaac. The popularity of such scriptural names in the Iranian biographical dictionaries shows a distinct pattern: During the eighth/second century they enjoy substantial popularity, amounting to some 30 percent of all names given by converts to Islam to their sons. However, as conversion to Islam accelerated during the ninth/ third century, this popularity quickly ebbed. Fathers became more interested in publicly affirming Islam by giving their sons names like Mohammad and Ahmad than in giving names that had earlier offered a sort of protective coloration—being either Muslim, Christian, or Jewish—when Muslims of Iranian ethnicity were few and far between. By 950/338 scriptural names had dropped to only 5 percent among converts' sons.[40] Though coincidence cannot be ruled out, the fact that the four scriptural names in table 1.4 show up in 27 percent of the 124 Arabic-named *fulanabads* on the list of most popular village names fits the earlier period far better than the later. This conclusion is reinforced by the fact that a number of quite uncommon Arabic *fulan* names included on the list of *fulanabads* in Qom (e.g., Ahwas—five villages, Shuʿaib—three villages) almost certainly relate to specific Arab leaders that are identified in the *Taʾrikh-e Qom* as being politically influential in the early decades of the century and even before.[41]

In light of the overall timetable of conversion and the onomastic evidence pointing to the late eighth/second to early ninth/third century as the most probable period of village genesis, the 80 percent predominance of Arabic names among the *fulanabad* villages of the Qom district points clearly to a disproportionate participation of Arabs and/or Iranian Muslim converts in the founding of new villages. A possible alternative explanation might be that the *fulanabad* pattern somehow in and of itself signified Muslim land ownership, and that Arabs or Muslim converts who acquired villages from Zoroastrian owners changed their old names to *fulanabad* names, conceivably as a symbolic effort to plant Islam on the land. This, however, is belied by the 20 percent of the *fulanabads* that do not have Arabic names. If the *fulanabad* pattern had indeed, in and of itself, signified Islam, its adoption by Zoroastrian landowners would have been nonsensical. Therefore, whatever the abundance of *fulanabads* signifies, it is something that relates much more strongly to the Arab/Muslim portion of the population than it does to the Iranian/Zoroastrian portion.

Several other place-name patterns corroborate this impression of a difference between Arab/Muslim agriculture and Iranian/Zoroastrian agriculture. One has already been mentioned, the twenty-nine exclusively Persian *fulanjirds*. Another concerns names beginning in *bagh*, or "garden." At least nineteen of the twenty-five "garden" locales contain Arabic *fulan* names (e.g., Bagh-e Idris, Bagh-e Abd al-Rahman). This makes them roughly 80 percent Arabic, just like the *fulanabads*. In addition, of the ten locales with names beginning in *sahra*ʾ, or "desert," only one is non-Arabic. The common denominator of the *fulanabad*, *bagh*, and *sahra*ʾ names is water. Gardens were commonly watered by qanat, and a similar qanat association for the village names compounded with *sahra*ʾ will be explained later. Most of the thirty-five *bagh* and *sahra*ʾ names, it should be noted, come from just three tax districts.

By contrast, another specialized term for a taxable locale is much more strongly associated with the Iranian–Zoroastrian sector. *Mazraʿeh,* meaning "cultivated field," but with an implication of dry farming, shows up seventy-seven times in plural or singular form either as a specifically named taxable

entity (e.g., Mazra'eh-ye Asmaneh, Mazra'eh-ye Binah) or as an appendage to
the name of a particular village (e.g., Binastar "and its cultivated fields" [*wa
mazare'iha*]). Only a quarter of these citations include Arabic names, however. Thirteen show up in the form of a *fulanabad* "and its cultivated field(s),"
and seven refer to individuals with Arabic names. Only one *mazra'eh* is listed
for the three districts that have a majority of the *bagh* and *sahra'* names.
From this one might surmise that some districts had a much higher concentration of Arab–Muslim villages than others.

The conclusion these number games lead to is that types of property
names that are strongly associated with qanats—*fulanabad*, *bagh*, and *sahra'*—
frequently incorporate Arabic personal names, whereas toponyms that are
unrelated to water (as well as those naming rivers and streams) rarely incorporate such names.

Our survey of the modern list of village names in the Qom region established
a strong correlation between the *fulanabad* name pattern and irrigation by
qanat. Projecting that correlation onto the (early) ninth-/third-century list
of *fulanabads*, we can most easily explain the 80 percent share of Arabic *fulans* by imagining a powerful wave of qanat building and village founding
carried out primarily by Arabs and/or Iranian converts to Islam. Is this a
sound hypothesis? The eleven-century gap between the modern gazetteer
and the Qom village list is a very long period, and naming practices could
have changed many times. So there is no way of proving directly that the *fulanabad*-qanat association has remained consistent throughout Iranian history. To make this association all but certain, we must turn to the economics
of cotton cultivation.

Hasan al-Qummi records the recollection of the old men of Qom that
before the coming of the Arabs, barley, carroway seeds, and saffron were the
only crops cultivated.[42] Whether this is literally true or not, it is unlikely, for
reasons already given, that any significant amount of cotton was cultivated in
Sasanid times. Tax records prove that this situation changed greatly some-
time after the conquest. The tax assessments per *jarib* for wheat, barley, and
cotton are shown in table 1.5.

TABLE 1.5    Tax Rates of Various Crops

| QOM | WHEAT | BARLEY | COTTON (ALL IRRIGATED) | WHEAT-TO-COTTON RATIO |
|---|---|---|---|---|
| Schedule I 804/188 | 15.16 dirhams | 15.16 dirhams | 38 dirhams | 1:2.5 |
| Schedule II 808/192 | 15.16 dirhams | 13.16 dirhams | 30 dirhams | 1:2 |
| Schedule VII 904/291 | 3.16 dirhams | 3.16 dirhams | 38 or 30 dirhams, depending on the district* | 1:12.5 or 1:10 |
| **MAH BASRA** | | | | |
| No date (the size of the *jarib* was presumably smaller in this district) | Unirrigated 6.06 | Unirrigated 4.50 | 15 dirhams | Unirrigated wheat—1:2.5 Unirrigated barley—1:3 |
| | Irrigated 1.08 | Irrigated 1.66 | | Irrigated wheat—1:15 Irrigated barley—1:9 |
| **HAMADAN** | | | | |
| No date, perhaps early 10th/4th century | Unirrigated 8.33 | Unirrigated 8.33 | 62 | Unirrigated grain—1:7.5 |
| | Irrigated 3.16 | Irrigated 3.16 | | Irrigated grain—1:18 |
| **SHIRAZ†** | | | | |
| Mid-10th/4th century, much larger *jarib* size | Unirrigated 190 | Unirrigated 190 | 257 1/3 dirhams | 1:1.35 |

* *Ta'rikh-e Qom*, 121.

† Ibn Hawqal, *Configuration de la Terre* (Kitab Surat al-Ard), tr. J. H. Kramers and G. Wiet (Paris: G.-P. Maissoneuve & Larose, 1964), 296.

Interpreting fixed tax rates, as opposed to a series of actual market prices, runs the risk of failing to consider unknown factors. Even so, looking at the ratios between the rates for grain and cotton, it is hard to imagine any factors that would substantially alter the conclusion that cotton farming was more profitable than grain farming. No farmer would have continued to plant cotton if his profit had been insufficient to pay his taxes, particularly at the beginning of the tenth/fourth century, when converting his irrigated acreage from cotton to wheat would have given him a tax rate ten to twenty times lower.

Another indicator of cotton's value may be found in the ratio between cotton and saffron. Saffron is now and probably always has been one of the world's most costly agricultural commodities, and one that is normally sold by the gram or the ounce. The hand labor of plucking the red top inch of the stigma of a small purple crocus is so enormous that saffron sells today for $45 to $60 an ounce. The rate for saffron on Tax Schedule 1 (804/188) is 15 dirhams per *jarib*, about the same as for wheat and barley, and less than half the rate for cotton. On Tax Schedule 7 (904/291) it is 62 dirhams, double the rate for cotton. By this comparative standard, which must reflect a greatly enhanced appreciation for saffron, the value of cotton fell somewhat during the course of the ninth/third century. But cotton continued to be a high-value crop, because by that time saffron was taxed at twenty times the rate for wheat and barley.

Was the apparent bonanza for cotton farmers in the Qom area in the ninth/third century as great as the one Egyptian or Carolina cotton farmers would enjoy in the nineteenth/thirteenth century? Probably not. It must be kept in mind that even if all the *fulanabad* villages grew cotton, they amounted to only 26 percent of the taxable locales around Qom. In terms of acreage, therefore, wheat and barley for local consumption doubtless continued to dominate Iranian agriculture by a wide margin. The cotton trade profited a relatively small number of growers. But because it was tied directly to cloth manufacturing and the export market, these growers played a major role in the urban and interregional commercial life of their districts.

A steady tax rate throughout the ninth/third century shows that cotton's profitability persisted. Soil depletion must have been a problem, as it is anywhere cotton is grown, but there was no shortage of unspoiled land if water could just be brought to it. Accounting for the steep decline in the taxation levels of wheat and barley from the beginning of the ninth/third to the middle of the tenth/fourth century is another matter. Particularly striking is the differential between rates for grain grown on irrigated as opposed to unirrigated land. One might suppose that the profitability of cotton would have prompted grain farmers to shift to the new crop, thereby reducing grain production and raising the market price of wheat and barley. Though no market prices that might prove this have been preserved, a plausible interpretation of the astoundingly low tenth-/fourth-century tax on irrigated grain fields is that the assessors who fixed the rates were bent on discouraging conversion to cotton by those wheat and barley farmers whose land was well enough watered to make this feasible.

Though the idea of using tax policy to discourage conversion from grain to cotton seems too modern for medieval times, exactly such a policy may have been prompted by a growing problem of sustaining burgeoning urban populations. If the cotton boom began, as we are hypothesizing, when desert lands that had previously been barren were first cultivated, then the acreage devoted to staple grains would not have been affected. Yet part of the agricultural labor force would have shifted to nonfood production. Moreover, as the boom continued, the coordinated growth of city-based textile production and marketing would have become one of the important factors contributing to the dramatic growth in urban population levels generally observed in the ninth/third and tenth/fourth centuries.[43] Rural–urban migration would thus have compounded the problem of rural workers shifting from food grain to cotton production by luring even more villagers away from the countryside completely. As a greater and greater proportion of Iran's working population took up residence in cities or devoted their labor to growing cotton, grain production seems to have become less and less adequate for supporting people who were no longer engaged in producing food.

I have argued in my book *Islam: The View from the Edge*[44] that precisely this pattern of imbalance between city size and rural food production made Iran vulnerable to severe food shortages and urban unrest in the eleventh/ fifth century, and I propose later in this book that a change in climate also contributed to a deteriorating food situation at that time. But the falling tax rates on grain during the preceding century may well have signaled an early awareness of this developing problem. Despite the suspiciously modern tenor of this sort of tax policy, it might be noted that in the nineteenth/thirteenth century, when Iran's leaders had no better understanding of the science of economics than their predecessors had had 1000 years earlier, a governor of Isfahan reacted to a spectacular rise in profits from growing poppies and exporting opium by requiring that farmers plant one *jarib* of grain for every four of poppies, lest food grains disappear from the market.[45]

Recall, however, that most grain farmers did not have the option of switching from wheat and barley to cotton. As already mentioned, wheat and barley are normally winter crops in Iran. They are planted in autumn, lie dormant over the winter, and sprout in the early spring. This agricultural cycle is deeply embedded in Iranian culture and is symbolized by the dish of wheat (or lentil) sprouts presented as part of the *haft sin* ("seven esses": *sabzeh* = green sprouts) ritual at the Iranian Nowruz, or New Year, festival, which takes place at the vernal equinox on March 21. Cotton, however, is a summer crop. It is normally planted in April, grows during the dry, torrid summer months, and is ready for harvest in early fall. In those parts of Iran where rain or snowfall alone, or rivers swollen by spring runoff, provided the moisture needed for cultivation, therefore, cotton could seldom be grown. Qanat irrigation, which provides a year-round steady flow from underground aquifers, was the key to cultivating cotton in the piedmont terrain characteristic of the Iranian plateau.

As we have seen, the evidence from toponyms and tax rates strongly suggests a wave of qanat building and village construction carried out by Muslim entrepreneurs. But this begs the question of what role qanat irrigation played in the pre-Islamic agricultural economy. Did roughly a third of the villages in Sasanid times have qanats as they did in the *Ostan-e Markazi* in the 1950s? Or were qanats used more for towns and gardens than for field crops? No direct answer to these questions can be advanced from the data at hand. However, there are two indirect indicators that suggest that qanats were much less common in preconquest villages than they became in later times, when urbanization and the textile industry made agriculture more profitable by drawing farmers into a market economy.

One indicator appears in table 1.5 in the data for the Hamadan/Mah Basra district west of Qom. Grain grown on irrigated land is taxed at a rate

that is between one seventh and one third of the rate imposed on unirrigated crops. This is the exact opposite of a general statement made by the
geographer Ibn Hawqal in discussing taxes in the southwestern province of
Fars: "On fields that receive water from rain, the tax is one third of what it
is for irrigated fields."[46] Because unirrigated lands normally yield smaller
crops than irrigated lands, Ibn Hawqal's statement makes good sense. The
Hamadan/Mah Basra rates, therefore, if they are not reported in error,
seem to represent a substantial incentive to get grain farmers to invest in
qanat irrigation. (In the 1950s most villages furnished with qanats grew
grain.) This hints at the likelihood that before the cotton boom, most grain
farmers practiced dry farming and did not make heavy investments in qanat
construction.

The second indirect indicator depends on the specific meaning of the
word *ba'ireh*, or "uncultivated." Lambton tells us that, "both in pre-Islamic
and Islamic times it was not uncommon for the underground water channels
(*kariz* = qanat) to dry up. Estates which had become waste-land (*dai'atha-ye
ba'ireh*) because of the drying up of a *kariz* are . . . mentioned in the *kharaj*
[tax] register for A.H. 345" (956–7).[47] If this understanding of the word *ba'ireh*
is correct, then a list of all the village names that are followed by that word
should help us. Out of the 1271 place-names given in the Qom tax registers,
thirty-three are described as *ba'ireh*: sixteen of these citations refer to *fulanabad* villages, and seventeen refer to non-*fulanabad* locales. Yet *fulanabad* villages account for only 26 percent of the 1271 names. Because the drying up of
qanats is a natural phenomenon caused by collapse, siltation, or changes in
the water table,[48] there is no reason to suppose that a qanat dug in the Sasanid
period to irrigate wheat or barley would have dried up either more or less
rapidly than one dug to irrigate cotton in the Islamic period. Randomness,
therefore, would dictate that if non-*fulanabad* villages were just as likely to
be irrigated by qanat as *fulanabad* villages, then the number of non-*fulanabads* listed as *ba'ireh* should be three times as great as the number of the *fulanabads*. The fact that the number of villages is essentially the same for the
two categories points to a greatly higher incidence of qanat irrigation in the
*fulanabad* villages.

These two indirect indicators reinforce the identification of *fulanabad*
villages with qanat irrigation. Given that 80 percent of the *fulanabads* were

named for Muslims, it is reasonable to conclude that most Zoroastrian village owners did not have the option of growing cotton. Their water supply
was not suitable. Of course, some evidently did act as entrepreneurs and did
establish new villages based on qanats. As we have seen, 20 percent of the *fulanabad* villages had non-Arabic names. But most seem to have stuck to the
lands that they owned before the conquest and to the agricultural techniques
of that period. This must have limited the opportunities for Arabs to buy
existing village estates, though there are instances of well-placed Muslims
marrying their sons to the daughters of Zoroastrian landowners who converted to Islam.[49] But the continuation of Zoroastrian landowning and agricultural patterns from the preconquest period also meant that Arabs or
nonlanded Iranian converts to Islam were the people most likely to have
sponsored the digging of qanats and the planting of cotton.

To summarize, although the exiguous and indirect character of the historical sources has rendered the preceding arguments sometimes convo-
luted and suppositious, taken altogether they strongly support the following
conclusions:

1. The interior plateau region of Iran began to experience a cotton boom of
   great magnitude in the early ninth/third century.
2. The boom was based on the founding of villages on lands that required
   qanat irrigation. (As the boom spread to Central Asia, other irrigation techniques prevailed.)
3. Muslims played the dominant role in founding these villages even though
   they amounted to no more than half the Iranian population by mid-
   century.
4. Zoroastrian village owners whose lands were inherited from the Sasanid
   period and were generally watered by other means did not share equally in
   the boom.

To those skeptically inclined readers who earlier felt unconvinced by arguments resting on occupational names among the religious elite of Nishapur,
reliance on data from a single district in north-central Iran may seem to viti-
ate these conclusions. Not only is Qom only a single district, but its political
history in the ninth/third century was atypical. Unlike most parts of Iran,

immigrant Arabs dominated the region, and Shi'ism became the prevailing form of Islam. The *Ta'rikh-e Qom* has much more to say about the political machinations of the major Arab families and about charges of unfair taxation than it does about village names and crops. It might also be noted that the rise of cotton farming in Nishapur, as indicated by the professional names of the ulama summarized in table 1.1, took place toward the end of the ninth/third century.

Though Nishapur ultimately became a larger city and a more important cotton center than Qom, two considerations make it likely that it became involved in the boom at a somewhat later date. First, Qom was much closer to Baghdad and the other cities of southern Iraq, which must have constituted the first major export market for Iranian cloth.[50] Second, the Arabs who dominated Qom came originally from Yemen, a land where cotton was a common crop in the pre-Islamic period. Nishapur did not have a large number of Yemeni settlers.

Compounding the difficulty of comparison, a list survives that names sixty-eight villages situated so near the pre-Islamic walled city of Nishapur that they eventually became engrossed into the expanding metropolis. The list contains fifteen *fulanabads*, which is close to the proportion for the Qom region. But only three begin with incontestably Muslim personal names. A fourth makes the list as follows: "the walled city (*shahrastan*) of Sabur [i.e., Shapur II, the Sasanid emperor who founded Nishapur] is now called Nasrabad." *Nasr* is an Arabic word that can indeed be used as a personal name, but its significance here comes from its meaning as a common noun meaning "victory." Evidently Nishapur's conquerors renamed the old walled city of the Sasanid shah "Victory-abad" in an effort to appropriate it as their own territory. Why are there so few Arabic *fulanabads*? Probably it is because digging qanats very close to an established city had less to do with agriculture than with bringing water to a rapidly growing urban population. In this, Muslims may have had no special or exclusive interest. The cotton fields that eventually contributed to Nishapur's reputation as a textile center were presumably established farther from town and involved Iranian converts to Islam more than Arab settlers.

# Chapter Two
## ISLAM AND COTTON

IN THE LAST CHAPTER I ARGUED that the economics of bringing new land under production and raising summer crops in qanat-irrigated fields made Iran's cotton boom possible in piedmont districts like Qom. But the boom affected nonpiedmont districts as well. The ninth-/third-century geographers who often list the notable products of different districts do not single out either Qom or Hamadan as major cotton-producing areas. Instead they mention Nishapur, Rayy, and Isfahan, the three largest cities of northern Iran, along with Bukhara and Samarqand in Uzbekistan, and Marv, which is today in southern Turkmenistan but was then considered, along with Nishapur, one of the capitals of the province of Khurasan. Geographically, Nishapur, Rayy, and Isfahan share the piedmont terrain of the Qom district and the eastern part of the Hamadan district, from which our tax data emanate. Agriculture in Marv, however, was based on canal irrigation on the lower reaches of the Murghab River, where it disappears into the Karakum desert. Farmers around Bukhara and Samarqand utilized the waters of the Zeravshan River. Both rivers drained the snow-capped mountains of Afghanistan and Tajikistan, which, unlike the much scantier snow cover of Iran, produced a perennial flow sufficient to irrigate summer crops like cotton. What all these districts had in common was a long, hot growing season; an abundant and steady water supply; and a growing community of Muslims. The first two of these elements speak for themselves. The third calls for examination, especially since cotton growing predated the Arab conquest of Central Asia but expanded greatly under Muslim rule.

Who grew the cotton? How was it marketed? Who bought it? Who turned it into cloth? Where was it sold? Why did a crop that was almost entirely unknown in Sasanid Iran become so phenomenally lucrative after the Arab conquest? And how was cotton connected with Islam?

A shift from questions of "what happened?" to questions of "who was involved and why?" necessitates a shift in data sources from the economic and geographic to the social and religious. The beginning of the last chapter tapped information from a biographical dictionary containing the names of the religious elite of Nishapur. Sources of this sort have more to tell us. Islamic biographical dictionaries vary greatly from region to region and century to century, but a number of those that deal with Iran during this period are quite similar in structure and consistent in content.[1] Each focuses on a single city with its surrounding region. And each includes 1000 or more biographical notices, alphabetically arranged, of religiously eminent Muslims, especially scholars who were involved in transmitting the traditions (*hadith*) of the Prophet and who were natives of or sojourners in that city.

As in the earlier discussion of cotton in Nishapur, the names of the biographical subjects will be our primary concern. Early Islamic naming practices could be quite complicated, but some names, called *nisbas*, or adjectives indicating a relationship, specified a person's occupation. Within the subset of biographical subjects whose names include mention of an occupation, some of the occupational *nisbas* were doubtless inherited from a father or grandfather, with the individuals themselves never practicing the trade indicated. Nevertheless, occupational names were not then frozen into immutable surnames the way Smith, Farmer, Cooper, and Sawyer are today. Anecdotal and literary sources often confirm that Ahmad the Baker did indeed bake bread and that Mohammad the Coppersmith did hammer out copper pans. One indirect confirmation of this statement comes from Sam Isaac Gellens's tabulation of occupational names on Egyptian tombstones, a presumably "democratic" (i.e., not obviously socially stratified) onomastic source.[2] Some of the most common trades—carpenter, fisher, saddler, milkman, and dyer—were too low in social status to show up on a parallel list Gellens compiled of occupational names among the Egyptian ulama. Had occupational names simply been inherited and the association with the actual trade lost, this would not have been the case. In addition, the fact that certain occupational epithets reflect clear geographical differences (*Khayyash*, or "dealer in coarse linen," shows up as a personal name in linen-producing Egypt but not in cotton-producing Khurasan, and vice versa for *Karabisi*, or "dealer in heavy cotton") reinforces the impression that these names are not entirely conventional but relate in many instances to the actual economic activities of a given region.

Two names will be the primary focus of our attention: *Qattan*, meaning "cotton grower" or "seller of raw cotton" (the word *cotton* in English is derived from Arabic *qutn*) and *Bazzaz*, meaning "dealer in cotton cloth." As table 2.1 shows, the ratio between these names in the biographical dictionaries of four Iranian cities is roughly one to one, but in the great Iraqi metropolis of Baghdad it is closer to five to one.[3]

The most straightforward reading of these figures is that in the cotton-producing areas of Isfahan, Nishapur, Qazvin (also a piedmont city), and Gorgan (on the low rainy plain at the southeast corner of the Caspian Sea) there was a near balance between growing cotton and selling cotton cloth. Moreover, both occupations were of sufficiently elevated status for people of religious distinction to include reference to them in their names. Indeed, for most of the chronological periods into which these four dictionaries are divided, Qattan and Bazzaz are among the three most frequently listed occupations. (*Tajir*, or "general merchant," is usually the third.)

The situation in Baghdad contrasts sharply with this. Dealers in cotton cloth far outnumber the cotton growers. The explanation for this difference

TABLE 2.1    Occupational names relating to fibers in biographical dictionaries

| CITY | COTTON CLOTH: BAZZAZ | COTTON AS A CROP: QATTAN | SILK: IBRISIMI, QAZZAZ, KHAZZAZ, HARIRI | WOOL: SAWWAF |
|---|---|---|---|---|
| Isfahan | 17 | 17 | 4 | 0 |
| Nishapur (al-Hakim) | 23 | 18 | 3 | 0 |
| Qazvin | 43 | 30 | 4 | 3 |
| Gorgan | 15 | 13 | 10 | 0 |
| Baghdad | 258 | 57 | 40 | 6 |

lies in the fact that, then as now, little cotton was grown in Iraq. Prior to large-scale flood control projects undertaken in the twentieth/fourteenth century, spring flooding caused by snow melt in the mountains of Turkey made the Tigris and Euphrates too unruly for summer cropping. The only exceptions to this seem to have been along the lengthy Nahrawan Canal, which channeled water from the Tigris into the farming countryside east of Baghdad, and in the Ahwaz region, today part of Iran, which received its irrigation water from the less tumultuous Karun River. These are the only two regions identifiable in the biographical dictionary of Baghdad as the home districts of people named Qattan. (That this name actually did mean a "grower or marketer of raw cotton" is apparent from the fact that several of the people named Qattan are described as living or working in the Dar al-Qutn, or House of Cotton, which seems to have been the warehouse building where cotton marketing was centered in Baghdad. *Daralqutni*, an uncommon personal name derived from this building, probably signifies the profession of cotton dealer as well.)

The great disproportion between cotton growers and cotton cloth merchants in Baghdad raises an obvious question: Assuming that the cloth merchants were so numerous because of a high demand for their goods (as opposed, say, to each Baghdad merchant having a smaller volume of business than his counterpart in Iran), where did they get their merchandise? Iraq itself clearly produced too little cotton to supply the Baghdad market. Egypt, the great cotton producer of modern times, then produced no cotton at all. Since ancient times, linen had been the everyday fabric worn by Egyptians, and Egyptian linen was widely exported. As for Syria, the geographers report that cotton was indeed grown in the area north of Damascus, and Syrian cottons played a minor role in Mediterranean trade; but there is no indication that Syrian cotton was exported to Baghdad.[4] Yemen, the only other cotton-producing area of the medieval Arab world, supplied the holy cities of Mecca and Medina, but it had only limited trade with Iraq. The conclusion that presents itself, therefore, is that most of the cotton cloth sold in Baghdad and other Iraqi cities like Kufa and Basra was imported from Iran, though India, a major cotton-producing region, cannot be entirely ruled out.

Baghdad alone constituted a huge market: a thriving caliphal capital that was five to ten times the size of the major Iranian cities. What Manchester was for the plantation owners of the American South, Baghdad seems to have been for the Iranian cotton industry, except that the Iranians shipped finished cloth to Iraq rather than raw cotton. This thriving trade with the caliphal center at last explains how Iran's cotton farmers could have earned enough from their crops to pay taxes at a rate two to ten times higher than that for staple grains at different points in the ninth/third century. But as we shall see, it also contributes to our understanding of the transformation of the Iranian plateau from an overwhelmingly rural land dominated by Sasanid regional barons to a land where flourishing cities became centers for the weaving and export of cloth, on the one hand, and for the growth of a specifically Muslim culture and scholarly community, on the other.

The skeptically inclined will again raise an eyebrow at the claim that significant variations in economic activities can be deduced from biographical dictionaries devoted primarily to religious scholars. At first glance, an argument of this sort seems a bit like trying to dissect the American national economy on the basis of the occupational names borne by college professors in *Who's Who in America*. But although the latter calculation would indeed be misguided, the relation between occupations and religious scholarship in early Islamic Iran is robust and significant.

The first hint of the relationship between religion and cloth can be found in the data on wool and silk presented in table 2.1. There is no question but that wool was common and ubiquitous throughout the Middle East in both the Sasanid and Islamic periods. Vast quantities of wool must have been marketed every year. Yet wool dealing is almost totally absent from the occupational names of religious scholars in Iran and Iraq. In part, this derives from the fact that wool came from the pastoral nomadic sector of the economy. What profit there was to be made from wool sales, therefore, went to individuals from the least educated and least literate stratum of society, or to brokers who associated with them and conveyed their products to market. To be sure, there were doubtless a few great wool wholesalers who were not themselves from pastoral backgrounds, but wool was also a crude fiber unsuited to the dignity of the religious elite. Like Weaver, Potter, and Fisher, occupational names that almost never appear in biographical dictionaries, the name *Sawwaf,* or "wool dealer," bespoke a trade that cast no credit on a person who aspired to be counted among the ulama. Since an occupational epithet was a completely optional part of a person's name, association with an undignified trade could easily be suppressed. To be sure, the association of wool, *suf* in Arabic, with poverty and abjection is commonly believed to be the source of the term *Sufi,* which denotes a current of Islamic mysticism that incorporated many esteemed ascetic practices and beliefs. Yet wearing wool to show one's humility was not at all the same as trading in wool.

If wool was humble, silk was the opposite. The aristocratic elite of the Sasanid era favored both silk cloth (*harir*) and figured silk brocade (*dibaj*). Evidence for this preference abounds in pictorial representations from that period and is also reflected in the Quran. In describing the bliss of Paradise, verse 23 of the *Surat al-Hajj* reads: "Allah will admit those who believe and work righteous deeds, to Gardens beneath which rivers flow: they shall be adorned therein with bracelets of gold and pearls; and their garments there will be of silk."

For Muslims, however, this vision of luxury was reserved for saved souls. The *hadith* of the Prophet are unequivocal in their condemnation of Muslim men wearing silk in this world. The *hadith* collection of al-Bukhari contains the following examples:

1. Abu ʿAmr or Abu Malik al-Ashʿari narrated that he heard the Messenger of God say: "From among my followers there will be some people who will consider illegal sexual intercourse, the wearing of silk, the drinking of alcoholic drinks, and the use of musical instruments as lawful. And [from them], there will be some who will stay near the side of a mountain, and in the evening their shepherd will come to them with their sheep and ask them for something, but they will say to him, 'Return to us tomorrow.' Allah will destroy them during the night and will let the mountain fall on them, and Allah will transform the rest of them into monkeys and pigs and they will remain so till the Day of Resurrection" [7:494].

2. Uqba b. ʿAmr narrated: "A silken *farruj* [a kind of shirt] was presented to the Messenger of God and he put it on and offered the prayer in it. When

he finished the prayer, he took it off violently as if he disliked it and said, 'This [garment] does not befit those who fear Allah!'" [7:693].

3. Abu 'Uthman al-Nahdi narrated: "While we were with 'Utba b. Farqad in Azerbaijan, there came 'Umar's letter indicating that the Messenger of God had forbidden the use of silk except this much. Then he pointed with his index and middle fingers. To our knowledge, by that he meant embroidery" [7:718].

4. Abu 'Uthman narrated: "While we were with 'Utba, 'Umar wrote to us: The Messenger of God said, 'There is none who wears silk in this world except that he will wear nothing of it in the Hereafter.' Abu 'Uthman pointed out with his middle and index fingers" [7:720].

5. Ibn Abi Laila narrated: "While Hudhaifa was at al-Mada'in, he asked for water whereupon the chief of the village brought him water in a silver cup. Hudhaifa threw it at him and said, 'I have thrown it only because I have forbidden him to use it, but he does not stop using it. The Messenger of God said, "Gold, silver, silk and *dibaj* are for them [unbelievers] in this world and for you [Muslims] in the Hereafter"'" [7:722].

6. Anas b. Malik narrated: "The Messenger of God said, 'Whoever wears silk in this world shall not wear it in the Hereafter'" [7:723].

7. Al-Bara' narrated: "The Messenger of God was given a silk garment as a gift, and we started touching it with our hands and admiring it. On that the Messenger of God said, 'Do you wonder at this?' We said, 'Yes.' He said, 'The handkerchiefs of Sa'd b. Mu'adh in Paradise are better than this'" [7:727].

8. Hudhaifa narrated: "The Messenger of God forbade us to drink out of gold and silver vessels, or eat from them, and also forbade the wearing of silk and *dibaj* or sitting on it" [7:728].

9. 'Ali b. Abi Talib narrated: "The Messenger of God gave me a silk suit. I went out wearing it, but seeing the signs of anger on his face, I tore it and distributed it among my wives" [7:731].

10. 'Abdullah b. 'Umar narrated: "'Umar saw a silk suit being sold, so he said, 'O Messenger of God! Why don't you buy it so that you may wear it when delegates come to you, and also on Fridays?' The Messenger of God said, 'This is worn only by him who has no share in the Hereafter.' Afterwards the Messenger of God sent to 'Umar a silk suit suitable for

wearing. 'Umar said to the Messenger of God, 'You have given it to me to wear, yet I have heard you saying about it what you said?' The Messenger of God said, 'I sent it to you so that you might either sell it or give it to somebody else to wear'" [24:5144].

The long-simmering scholarly debate over whether *hadith* such as these—or indeed any *hadith*—stem from the seventh-/first-century milieu of the Prophet and his Companions in Mecca and Medina or whether some or all of them emanate from an Iraqi milieu of the late eighth/second century need not detain us. Religious disapproval of Muslim men wearing silk was absolute whether it was first articulated in remote western Arabia, where silk garments were rare, costly, and admired (see *hadith* 7, 9–10 in the preceding list), or whether it reflects a desire to avoid the luxurious practices of the non-Arab elite that the Muslim armies encountered during the conquests that began after Muhammad's death (see *hadith* 3, 5).

If silk was forbidden, what was a pious Muslim man to wear? Maureen Fennell Mazzaoui, the historian of the transfer of the Middle Eastern cotton industry to Italy in the twelfth/sixth century, provides the following overview:

The Arab conquest marked a complete reorientation of Near Eastern and Mediterranean commerce, including the cotton trade. The Arabs were the first people in the Near East to adopt cotton on a wide scale for ordinary clothing and other purposes . . . Indian cloth was from earliest times an important object of Arab trade while the Arabian peninsula [notably Yemen—RWB] was one of the first areas outside India to which the cotton plant was brought.

The widespread use of cotton clothing among the Arab tribes dates back certainly to the time of Mohammed and probably much earlier. The prophet himself is reported to have worn a white cotton shirt with trousers, presumably of the same material, covered by a woolen cloak. The cloth may have come from Oman and the Yemen where there was an old and well-established cotton manufacture. The same costume, which undoubtedly reflected the simple mode of dress already prevalent in the area, was worn by the caliphs Omar and Ali and their followers. This form of attire was consonant with Mohammed's pronouncements on modesty and the avoidance of ostentation in dress which became the basis for a system of sumptuary legislation worked out by Islamic jurists. Islamic law prohibited the use of gold, silk, or other luxury materials in masculine attire. Cotton, linen, and wool were acceptable fabrics. The approved colors were black and white.[5]

What this skillfully crafted and generally unimpeachable summary fails to observe is that the plain-dressing Arab tribes constituted but a small and dispersed minority within the vast realm of the caliphate established by their feats of arms. The transfer of the clothing preferences of these Arabs to what in time becomes a vastly larger population of non-Arab converts to Islam is what needs examination. How do Arab tastes become Muslim tastes, particularly when the elite of the non-Arab peoples had been indulging a taste for silk brocade for many centuries?

Oddly enough, neither cotton nor linen nor wool is referred to more than a few times in the *hadith*. Condemning silk called for the moral authority of the Prophet; approving other fibers apparently did not. What references there are sometimes specify the place of origin. For linen it is Egypt:

11. Dihya b. Khalifa al-Kalbi narrated: "The Messenger of God was brought some pieces of fine Egyptian linen and he gave me one and said: Divide it into two; cut one of the pieces into a shirt and give the other to your wife for a veil" [*Sunan* of Abu Da'ud, 32:4104].

For cotton it is Yemen. *Al-Muwatta'*, a compendium of *hadith* by Malik b. Anas, contains the following:

12. Yahya related to me from Malik, from Hisham b. 'Urwa, from his father, from 'A'isha, the wife of the Messenger of God, that the Messenger of God was shrouded in three *sahuli* white cotton garments, none of which was a long shirt or turban. [*Sahuli* refers to pure white cotton cloth that came from Sahul, a town in Yemen.]

13. Yahya related to me from Malik that Yahya b. Sa'id said that he had heard that when Abu Bakr al-Siddiq was ill, he asked 'A'isha, "How many

shrouds did the Messenger of God have?" and she replied, "Three *sahuli* white cotton garments."

As for wool, there is little to be found in the way of Prophetic endorsement:

14. 'A'isha, the Mother of Believers, narrated: "I made a black cloak for the Messenger of God and he put it on; but when he sweated in it and noticed the odor of the wool, he threw it away [*Sunan* of Abu Da'ud, 32:4063].

On the matter of color, several *hadith* confirm that white was preferred, though black became the officially favored color of the Abbasid dynasty that seized power in 750/132:

15. Ibn al-'Abbas narrated: "I heard the Messenger of God saying, 'Put on white clothes because they are the best; and use them for shrouding your dead'" [al-Tirmidhi and Abu Da'ud].
16. Samura narrated: "The Messenger of God said, 'Wear white clothes because they are the purest and they are closest to modesty; and shroud the dead in it" [i.e., white cloth; al-Nasa'i and al-Hakim].

Looking at *hadith* evidence as a whole, the strident disapproval of silk and silk brocade and the somewhat lukewarm piety attached to white linen and cotton, both for garments and for shrouds (one could also add for pilgrimage costume) raise the likelihood that the early Islamic period was less one of easy dissemination to the entire Muslim community of Arab tribal clothing preferences than one of dueling aesthetics in those territories that had been part of the Sasanid empire. Silk brocade continued to stand for aristocracy, wealth, and luxury; and names for specific types of silk far outnumber words for cotton and linen fabrics in narrative sources emanating from Muslim ruling circles.[6] But silk also marked its wearer as sentimentally attached to Sasanid aesthetics and an insincere Muslim to boot. By contrast, plain white cotton (or linen in Egypt) signaled sincere Islam and marked its wearer as one who shared in the aesthetic of the conquering Arabs.

Xinru Liu has argued the opposite on the basis of an abundance of evidence showing that silk was continuously appreciated and consumed in ruling circles. "The thrust of Islamic sumptuary rules [i.e., prohibitions of silk] was not to demarcate the ruling from the ruled, but to facilitate a compromise between religious asceticism and hedonism in Arabian traditional culture."[7] Liu's descriptions of caliphal treasures and gifts and anecdotes about luxurious living cannot be gainsaid. Silk continued to be purchased and worn. But presenting an interpretive choice between distinguishing "the ruling and the ruled" and compromising between "religious asceticism and hedonism" ignores the evolving relationship between Muslims and non-Muslims.

If all Muslims fell into the category of rulers and all non-Muslims into the category of the ruled, or alternatively, if everybody professed Islam but split into two parties, one favoring ascetic and the other hedonistic lifestyles, Liu might have a point. In fact, however, the Muslims evolved from a small Arab minority governing a vast number of non-Arab non-Muslims into a society in which Islam was the common religion of rulers and ruled alike. It is unrealistic and, as we shall see, contrary to the historical evidence, to think that sumptuary prohibitions maintained a constant meaning throughout that evolution.

In the earliest period, it is not unreasonable to see the clash between Muslim and non-Muslim styles in the public arena as part of a policy formally distinguishing the rulers from the ruled. The Pact of ʿUmar, a document of somewhat uncertain date, purports to specify practices permitted to Christians living under Muslim rule in Syria.[8] Among other things, the Christians who are presented as signatory to the document affirm that: "We shall not seek to resemble the Muslims by imitating any of their garments, the *qalansuwa* [a skullcap or fez], the turban [usually cotton, linen, or silk], footwear, or the parting of the hair." This mirror image of the Muslim ban on silk—"silk and *dibaj* are for them [unbelievers] in this world and for you [Muslims] in the Hereafter"—can plausibly be interpreted as reflecting a desire by the ruling Muslims to retain their visible distinctiveness at a time when they were a small ruling minority. One might look for comparison to the Manchu insistence during the Qing dynasty that ethnic Chinese men wear a queue, or to the various clothing codes separating Jews from Christians at different periods of European history, or to the contrast between the sumptuous dress of Catholic Cavaliers and the unadorned clothing of Protestant Dissenters during the English Revolution.

Although the provenance of the Pact of ʿUmar is questionable, two anecdotes firmly anchored in early tenth-/fourth-century writings tend to support this interpretation. In one, an Umayyad prince fleeing the downfall of his dynasty in 750/132 is said to have reached Nubia (northern Sudan) and to have there entertained a visit from a local king. The local king refused to sit on the carpet laid out for him because he wished to be humble before God. Then he asked about the Umayyads' blameworthy practices, such as drinking wine and wearing sumptuous garments: "'Why,' proceeded the king, 'do you wear brocade and silk and gold, in spite of the prohibitions of your Book and your religion?' I retorted: 'As power fled from us, we called upon the support of alien races who have entered our faith and we have adopted these clothes from them.'"[9]

The other anecdote concerns al-Afshin, the hereditary ruler of a small principality in Tajikistan who wielded enormous power under the Abbasid caliph al-Muʿtasim (r. 833–842/217–227) through his military prowess and command over troops from Central Asia. When he was accused of being an insincere Muslim, for which he was eventually put to death, the court was told that in private he had once said: "Truly I have given in to these people [the Arabs] in everything I hated, even to the extent that because of them I have eaten oil and ridden camels and worn sandals. But not a hair has fallen from me!" Meaning that he had not used depilatories nor been circumcised.[10]

On the one hand, a fallen eighth-/second-century prince says that foreigners prevailed on his family to abandon the pure Arab ways; on the other, a ninth-/third-century Iranian prince serving a Muslim ruler testifies that he has abandoned his own traditions and adopted odious Arab customs. The former anecdote fits better the Abbasid period, when Persian styles prevailed in Baghdad and when the text containing the anecdote was composed. Unlike the Abbasids, the Umayyads never relied on "alien races." The latter story is equally dubious because it is part of a calumnious accusation. But both of them concur with the Pact of ʿUmar in affirming the symbolic importance of costume—headdress and footwear in the Pact, brocade and sandals in the anecdotes—in distinguishing ruling Arabs and subject non-Arabs. However contrived and ahistorical each story may be, both reflect a concern for personal appearance that must have seemed realistic to those who read them.

As already shown, the religious elite themselves had far greater involvement with cotton than with silk, despite the continuing popularity of the latter. As for those ulama who did deal in silk, there is no way of telling whether the consumers they catered to were men or women. The latter were clearly permitted to wear silk garments:

> 17. Ali b. Abi Talib narrated: "The Messenger of God took silk and held it in his right hand, and took gold and held it in his left hand and said: both of these are prohibited to the *males* of my community" [*Sunan* of Abu Da'ud, 32:4046, emphasis added].

This allowance probably derives from the fact that the silks worn by women were seldom seen outside the home because women covered themselves, usually with plain cotton, linen, or wool when they went out in public. The same situation continues today in Saudi Arabia and the Islamic Republic of Iran and among pious women in many other countries. Thus the wearing of silk by women at home would not have detracted from the visual contrast between austere Arab/Muslim dress and luxurious Sasanid/Zoroastrian dress in the public arena.

In table 2.1 the number of silk dealers ranges between 5 percent and 12 percent of the total number of cotton merchants (Qattan + Bazzaz) in three of the four Iranian cities; The ratio in Baghdad, whence much of the information about silk fabrics emanates, is 12 percent. In quantity if not in luxury, therefore, cotton greatly exceeded silk, at least in shops run by families that included notable religious figures. Even in Gorgan, which was the only one of the five cities to be famous for producing silk locally, there were three ulama cotton growers and cotton cloth merchants for every dealer in silk.

It is true, of course, that religious disapproval of wearing silk may have rendered the trade undesirable for some ulama, thus skewing samples drawn from biographical dictionaries of ulama. But there is no ignoring the favor that the caliphal governments accorded to the cotton and linen industries in their official establishment of factories for manufacturing *tiraz*. *Tiraz* was a

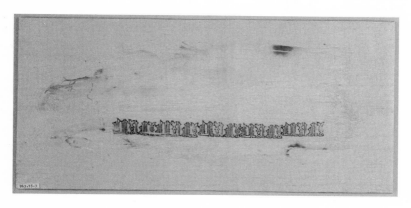

FIGURE 2.1.    Tiraz-style cotton textile with printed rather than embroidered calligraphy.
(By permission of the Royal Ontario Museum.)

fabric made of plain linen or cotton decorated only by a narrow woven or
embroidered band of ornamental Arabic writing (see fig. 2.1). The calligraphy
was invariably in silk. This explains the exceptions to the general prohibition
on wearing the luxury fabric mentioned in *hadith* 3 and 4: the "middle and
index fingers" denote the width of the band of *tiraz* calligraphy.[11] The reason
for the caliphs establishing factories for *tiraz* production was to provide a
special fabric for robes of honor granted as gifts to officials and favorites. The
calligraphy usually contained the name of the caliph.

Not only was *tiraz* produced in government factories, but a number of religious scholars had names associated with its manufacture, to wit, Mutarriz
or Tirazi. Upward of 1000 examples of *tiraz* still survive in museums, mostly
in the form of calligraphic bands that have been cut from the cloth they once
bordered. Yet even though the ground cloth has mostly been discarded, it is
clear from these specimens that the calligraphic band normally appeared at
the edge of a piece of plain or simply striped cloth large enough to be tailored
into a floor-length garment. Linen is by far the most common ground fiber in
these extant examples because most of them come from Egypt, where climatic
conditions favor the preservation of organic materials in archaeological excavations. But the near absence of the name Kattan, or linen dealer, in the biographical dictionary of Baghdad, where *tiraz* consumption was concentrated,
suggests that cotton was the common ground cloth in Iraq and Iran.

By ignoring the ground fabric and considering *tiraz* solely as a component of the silk trade in the Islamic world, Xinru Liu misrepresents an industry in which weavers produced many yards of ground fabric, whether cotton
or linen, to provide the background for just a few spools of silk thread.[12] *Tiraz* is at the heart of Liu's putative compromise between "religious asceticism
and hedonism" because it supposedly allowed people to avoid the "hedonism" of all-silk garments while relieving them of the "asceticism" of draping
their bodies with unornamented fabrics. (Wearing *mulham*, a fine textile
woven of both cotton and silk, provides a better example of this combination.) A more plausible interpretation is that rulers who coveted silk garments and fabrics for themselves granted just a touch of silken luxury to
those whom they favored with a robe of honor (*khil'a*). Beneath this *noblesse
oblige*, they were in fact underwriting the production of the finest cotton and
linen fabrics while observing the spirit of the religious prohibition of silk.

The dueling aesthetics represented by Sasanid brocade (*dibaj*) and Abbasid *tiraz* have left a trace in another area of manufacturing: ceramics. A
type of ninth–tenth-/third–fourth-century pottery known as "Nishapur
ware" or "Samarqand ware" constitutes a ceramic equivalent of *tiraz* (fig. 2.2).[13]
The potter coated a plate or shallow dish made of red clay with a thin layer
of pure white clay known as a "slip." Ornamental Arabic calligraphy was
then painted in black or aubergine on top of the slip around the rim of the
dish, and sometimes in a single line across the center as well. The calligraphy is difficult to decipher and usually devoted to moralistic aphorisms
(e.g., "Your modesty keep to yourself; behold, my actions prove my generosity" or "He who professes the faith will excel; and to whatever you accus-
tom yourself you will grow accustomed").[14] Assuming that the dishes,
which were made in vast quantity, were actually used for serving meals, it
was probably deemed improper to place food on the name of God or on an
actual Qur'anic quotation. Known to art historians as "slip-painted ware,"
this austere white pottery with aubergine calligraphy around the rim was
produced in Nishapur and Samarqand—both, not coincidentally, major
cotton-producing cities—and exported to other lands. The inscriptions on
this pottery were always in Arabic, despite Persian being the common language of the cities where it was made and Arabic being the language that
was the exclusive attainment of Arab immigrants and of the learned elite of
Iranian converts to Islam.

FIGURE 2.2.    Example of Nishapur slip-painted ware. (By permission of Louvre/Art
Resource, NY.)

A nearly contemporary pottery style in Nishapur, known to art historians
as "buff ware," contrasts strikingly with this slip-painted ware in that it pre-
serves the imagery and styles associated with the pre-Islamic landed aristocracy
(fig. 2.3). Many pieces—deep bowls for the most part—show birds and animals
or geometric patterns. But the occasional figurative design picks up hunting
and banqueting motifs from Sasanid silver feasting vessels. The men depicted
wear form-fitting brocade tunics with full skirts over boots and amply cut trousers, sometimes with a short cape added. Though these motifs are pre-Islamic
and early specimens of buff ware have been found at Sasanid excavation levels
at Marv, they seem for the most part to date from the ninth/third century in

FIGURE 2.3.    Example of figurative buff ware from Nishapur. (By permission of Islamic Art
Berlin/Art Resource, NY.)

Nishapur and to vanish in the eleventh/fifth century.[15] Though these two pottery styles overlap at specific excavation sites in the ruins of Nishapur, the popularity of the calligraphic slip-painted ware seems to diminish over time relative to the buff ware with Sasanid-era figurative designs.[16] We shall return to
this chronological succession of styles in considering the waning of the cotton
boom in chapter 3. Their contribution for the discussion here is to give another
example of how the balance between visual motifs—Muslim vs. non-Muslim,
Arab vs. Persian, elite vs. common—evolved over time.

    In two important areas of daily urban life, then, clothing styles and dining
styles (the different vessel shapes surely imply different dinner menus) there

was a clear clash between a Sasanid visual aesthetic and an Islamic visual aesthetic. As the politically dominant minority, Arabs and Muslim converts sought to assert their place in the public arena through visual symbolism. For Muslims to persevere with their distinctive look they had to institute changes in production, marketing, and technology. This has long been recognized with respect to pottery because so many distinctive specimens have survived the centuries, and because there are great stylistic and technical differences between Sasanid and Islamic ceramics. Pots made before the Arab conquest were mostly unglazed, or glazed in a monochrome green. In neither case was there an effort to imitate the silver and gold feasting vessels of the Sasanid aristocracy. By contrast, wares of the Muslim period show great variety and technical innovation, including imitation Tang Chinese splash-painted ware alongside the types already mentioned. Evidently the urban market for better-quality ceramics grew and potters developed new techniques and designs to supply it. Meanwhile the aristocratic market for precious plates and goblets waned. The evidence from place-names, personal names, and tax assessments has shown us that parallel innovations took place in the clothing industry.

To dress, eat, and ornament their homes in the Muslim style, the Arabs and Iranian converts of the ninth/third and, to a lesser degree, tenth/fourth centuries both fostered and patronized new forms of agricultural and industrial production. In the process they transformed the Iranian highlands from a rural land of autarkic villages traversed by luxury trade routes from China to a land of burgeoning cities producing cloth and high-quality ceramics for local consumption and export. The profits of trade financed the development of a distinctively Islamic urban society. Therefore, it is entirely appropriate that 80 percent of the *fulanabad* villages listed in the *Ta'rikh-e Qom* have Arabic names and that cotton production correlates so positively with the occupational names used by Muslim religious scholars. Despite the silken luxury of the caliphal court, in Iran Islam meant cotton, and cotton meant Islam—at least in the ninth/third century.

It is no coincidence that the people who transmitted (and possibly in some cases invented) the *hadith* prohibiting the wearing of silk were themselves often involved in the cotton trade. Conversion to Islam gained momentum in Iran in the middle of the ninth/third century. From a cotton grower's perspective, every new convert was a potential customer. New Muslims emulated the way of life manifested by the Arabs and sought to distinguish themselves from the Zoroastrian, Christian, or Jewish communities they were leaving behind. Not only were they inclined to swathe themselves in cotton gowns and turbans, but they would have purchased cotton cloth for their tightly wrapped burial shrouds, unlike the Zoroastrians whose corpses were covered in white for funerary purposes but eventually laid out naked in Towers of Silence (*dakhmas*) to be consumed by vultures.[17] For some Iranian Muslims, *karbas*, a heavy-duty cotton fabric similar to canvas, became synonymous with "burial shroud."[18] Needless to say, the domestic market for cotton generated by conversion to Islam in Iran was augmented by the growth of the convert population in Iraq, which created a demand for imported cotton goods that the well-established caravan routes leading from Iran and Central Asia were ideally situated to supply, particularly after the cotton boom reached the latter region.

In Iran there is a strong likelihood that the entrepreneurs who created new villages for growing cotton saw their own villagers as potential customers. A model of how this may have occurred can be found in Richard Eaton's *The Rise of Islam and the Bengal Frontier, 1204–1760*.[19] Eaton puts forward a persuasive and well-documented explanation for the dramatically successful spread of Islam in east Bengal, today the country of Bangladesh. In outline, he argues that Mughal sultans made land grants to government officials, who in turn contracted with entrepreneurs to convert jungle and woodland into rice paddies. These entrepreneurs, who were mostly but not exclusively Muslim, engaged local people to clear the jungle, build a village, and cultivate rice. When the entrepreneurs were Hindu, the resulting villages became Hindu. When they were Muslim, the villages became Muslim. Yet the local people who were recruited for the jungle clearing and rice planting were more often than not neither Hindu nor Muslim before becoming enmeshed in the land development scheme. Rather, they identified with local or tribal deities that were not associated with any literate religious tradition. As a result of village entrepreneurship triggering a large-scale change in religion, east Bengal became overwhelmingly Muslim in spite of its comparatively late incorporation into the Mughal Empire and a relative paucity of Muslim religious scholars and mosques.

Although Eaton suggests that this association between religious change and agricultural development could be a product of the economic advance represented by the transition from forest foraging to rice growing, or of the simultaneous transition from an illiterate to a literate religious tradition, the village scale of the transition may have been an equally important factor. In Malcolm Gladwell's *The Tipping Point*, a popular presentation of several sociological approaches to the problem of sudden change, the point is made, with sundry examples, that uniformity of outlook and fruitful interaction within a group arise most readily when the population of the group does not exceed approximately 150.[20] Looking at east Bengal with this observation in mind, one might wonder whether the scale at which the land development took place, namely, the small agricultural village, in and of itself contributed substantially to the homogeneity that subsequently appeared in social and religious outlook, whether Muslim or Hindu. In such a small community, there may have been neither room for nor tolerance of religious diversity. This would explain why the religion of the entrepreneur determined the religion of the village. By comparison, the larger populations of towns and cities could have more readily retained or sustained religious variety.

I am only guessing that the average size of the new rice villages in east Bengal fell roughly into the range suggested by Gladwell. But for Iran, even in the 1950s, 150 souls was fairly close to the average village size—and for a good reason.[21] In a village watered by qanat, the rate of flow from the underground canal strictly limited the area that could be farmed, and therefore the quantity of food that could be produced. This lack of elasticity meant that natural population growth required the building of new villages or migration to a city. It seems likely, therefore, that the Muslim entrepreneurs who established cotton villages in the ninth/third century functioned analogously to the village entrepreneurs whose activities Eaton documented in east Bengal. That is to say, if the founder of a new *fulanabad* village in the Qom district happened to be a Muslim, as 80 percent seemingly were, then in recruiting workers he would either have required them to become Muslims or have prevented them from continuing in their previous faiths by the social pressures inherent in such small communities.

An East Bengal-style conversion mechanism of this sort would directly link the growth of the Iranian Muslim population to cotton farming and help explain why Iran seems to have converted more rapidly, particularly in urbanizing districts, than various other provinces conquered by the Arabs in the seventh/first century.[22] It would further provide an economic motivation for Islam penetrating the countryside around the Arab governing and garrison nodes as they evolved into regional marketing and manufacturing centers. Finally, it would help explain the persistence of non-Islamic beliefs in parts of Iran that were less amenable to the growing of cotton, such as the Alborz and Zagros mountains in the north and west and the torrid, waterless lands of the far south.

These suppositions cannot be directly confirmed, but the institution of "labor teams" lends them some credence. Javad Safinezhad, the previously mentioned Iranian geographer who demonstrated that the "labor team," or *boneh,* system of village organization almost perfectly overlaps the parts of Iran that irrigate with qanats, called his book on the subject *Boneh* because that is the term currently in use in the area of Iran around Tehran. But he observes that in other parts of Iran other terms are used. One of these terms is *sahra'*, and the region where it is in use is Khurasan, the center of the early Islamic cotton boom.[23]

One might well ask whether it makes sense to pursue a technical term attested in the twentieth/fourteenth century back to an early Islamic text such as the *Ta'rikh-e Qom*, but even on the face of it, the term *sahra'* appears antique. More commonly spelled "sahara" in English, it is the Arabic word for "desert," and Arabic has not been commonly used in Khurasan for more than 1000 years. Moreover, Persian has its own word for "desert," *biyaban*, literally "place without water," and hardly needs to borrow from the Arabs in this particular. Thus it seems more than likely that the use of *sahra'* to mean "labor team" dates to a period when Arab influence was high.

Assuming that it does, we suggest that it is connected with the ten taxable locales in the pattern of *sahra-ye fulan*, ostensibly "the 'desert' of so-and-so," listed in the Qom tax schedules and briefly mentioned in the previous chapter. In nine of those ten locales, the *fulan* component was an Arabic Muslim name. If the word *sahra'* were to be taken literally, the fact that these "deserts" were all named for Muslims would be decidedly anomalous. As we have seen, the only other place-name types around Qom that can be specifically identified as Muslim are *bagh-e fulan*, or "garden of so-and-so," with nineteen out of twenty-five names being Muslim, and the *fulanabad* villages themselves, eight out of ten of which were named for Muslims. In both of these comparative cases, the names can be plausibly associated with qanat irrigation. Moreover, the pattern *biyaban-e fulan*, which would be the Persian equivalent of *sahra-ye fulan*, never occurs as a place-name.

The word *sahra'* as it appears among the Qom place-names, probably refers to a specific piece of "desert" (i.e., a tract of uncultivable arid land that was made arable by digging a qanat). *Sahra-ye fulan* would thus denote the same thing as the much more common *fulanabad*. Twisting a foreign word for "desert" into a word for "cultivable land," moreover, provides a plausible route by which the same word has come to mean "field" in modern Persian and "work team" in the province of Khurasan.

If work teams did already exist in the ninth/third century, it would help explain how the entrepreneurs of the new cotton villages recruited their labor force. Membership in a work team that was guaranteed a fixed portion of the proceeds from a highly marketable crop may have been a very attractive proposition, even if the qanat owner made settlement in his village conditional upon at least nominal acceptance of the Islamic religion.

An impressionistic narrative of how the plateau region of Iran developed over the three centuries following the Arab conquest will draw together the arguments of the past two chapters and set the stage for the discussion to come of the near disappearance of cotton in the eleventh/fifth century. The economic basis of Iranian society remained rural and agricultural in the aftermath of the Arab conquests. The *dihqans*, the aristocratic landowners who survived the conquests and continued to reside in their country seats, also continued to provide local order and security. As before, they supported themselves from the surplus production of grain-producing villages that they either owned or had rights to. Some of them also helped collect taxes for the new caliphal government.

By the beginning of the ninth/third century, after 150 years of unsettled times marked by military expeditions from Iraq and the implantation of Arab garrisons, Muslim Arabs, including influential Yemeni families with knowledge of cotton growing, began to develop the economy in new directions. A very small number of non-Arab Muslim converts joined in this endeavor. These Muslim entrepreneurs had abundant financial means derived from war booty, local retention of tax revenues, and the conversion into coin of treasure seized from the Sasanian royalty, the higher aristocracy, and the Zoroastrian fire temples. But for the most part, they did not own farmland.

Islamic law, based ostensibly on the traditions of the Prophet, made it possible for a Muslim to gain freehold ownership of land through the process of bringing dead land (*ard al-mawat*) into production. Iran provided unique opportunities for this because of the indigenous qanat technology that made it possible to irrigate desert land throughout the piedmont districts that ringed the interior of the plateau. But qanats were expensive to build, which made it uneconomical to grow wheat and barley, the staple crops of the Sasanid era. So the entrepreneurs who built the qanats and established villages on the newly arable land turned to summer cropping, for which their year-round water supply afforded a competitive advantage. Their crop of choice was cotton, which could not be grown on land that depended solely on winter precipitation and was afflicted with extreme dryness in the summer.

Cotton fit perfectly into Muslim efforts to make their rule distinctive. A competition developed between the lifestyle preferred by the old Sasanid elite and that preferred by the small minority of Arab intruders and their convert allies. The Muslims promoted the wearing of plain white, or sometimes colored or striped clothing, a preference based on Arab traditions that dated either to the time of Muhammad or, less likely, to the period after the conquests, to justify the new lifestyle distinction between Muslim and non-Muslim.

Nevertheless, the Sasanid-era preference for silk brocade with figural designs continued to have great appeal, as can be seen in the luxury consumption of the caliphal court at the elite level and in the motifs on Nishapur's buff ware at the popular level. Though tailoring practices have not been discussed in detail, this too became an area of dueling aesthetics. Arab tastes favored draped rather than fitted garments: gowns, robes, turbans, kaffiyehs, and so on. The rival Sasanid-era wardrobe featured tunics with closely fitted bodices, short capes, and baggy trousers.

Muslims who were known for their piety or religious scholarship were active in developing the summer cropping of cotton. This is apparent from the comparison between occupational names among the ulama of four Iranian cities and Hayyim Cohen's independent survey of medieval Muslim religious dignitaries derived from geographically unrestricted compilations. The percentage of Iranian ulama engaged specifically in the cotton trade was almost twice as great as that for all textile dealers taken together in the general survey. Growing cotton and marketing cotton cloth became integral to ulama life, and they endorsed it religiously by teaching that it was sinful to wear silk. To this day cotton gowns and turbans in plain white, black, or brown constitute the standard dress of Iran's ulama.

It is also probable that the Muslim cotton entrepreneurs insisted that the farmers who settled in the villages that they founded adhere, at least nominally, to the Muslim faith. They had the money to entice laborers to leave their existing villages and join the work teams of the new villages. And the profitability of the new crop probably assured the labor force that they would enjoy an improved standard of living. For many, affirming membership in the Muslim community, which then required little in the way of knowledge of Islam, may have been only a minor inconvenience. Moreover, if Zoroastrian landowners had a traditional right, even a right sanctioned by Zoroastrian law, to demand that workers lured away by the new cotton economy return to their former villages, conversion to Islam, even in nominal terms, would have made such a right difficult to enforce.

In this fashion the cotton industry contributed to Islam's rapid spread in the rural districts close to key Arab governing and garrison centers. During the ninth/third and early tenth/fourth centuries, these centers developed into full-fledged cities in one of the most striking episodes of urbanization in world history. As the first major commodity ever to be produced and fabricated in Iran for large-scale export to other regions, primarily Iraq, cotton was a primary driver of this development. The bandwagon growth through conversion of the Muslim communities of Iran and Iraq provided an expanding market for domestic consumption and export, thus bringing great wealth to the cotton entrepreneurs, including many religious scholars. The consistently high taxation rate for cotton confirms this.

A contemporary anecdote from Isfahan reflects the assumption people made that a caravan traveler with a load of cloth could be indistinguishable from a religious scholar traveling to collect the *hadith* of the Prophet. The grandson of a noted *hadith* scholar was journeying with his uncle on the road to Nishapur. When they stopped at a certain well, the uncle recalled encountering an old camel-puller during a stop at the same well on an earlier trip. The camel-puller had told him the following story:

> I was on a caravan from Khurasan with my father, and when we came to this place, there were forty bales done up as camel loads. We thought they were woven cloth. There was also a small tent with an old man [*shaikh*] in it. (He was, in fact, your father.) Some of us asked about the bales, and he said: "This commodity [in those bales] is one that is sadly rare in these times. It is the *hadith* of the Messenger of God, prayers and peace be upon him."[24]

The cotton boom did not affect all parts of the country equally. Areas that were less suited to cotton production because of torrid temperature, lack of water, or mountainous terrain lost some of the prominence they had had in pre-Islamic times. In their place, Khurasan, the plains at the southeast corner of the Caspian Sea, and the inland slopes of the Zagros and Alborz mountains became more prosperous and developed a robust urban culture. These regions are still today the best suited for growing cotton. Isfahan, Rayy, Nishapur, and Marv (then part of Khurasan) swelled in population and developed extensive trade relations with regions beyond the plateau. Bukhara and Samarqand shared this prominence, but they were already substantial cities and the capitals of local principalities in the pre-Islamic period. Where earlier they were known for silk, now cotton was their main export.

A case in point is a large piece of pre-Islamic silk in the collegiate church of Notre-Dame de Huy in Belgium. A Sogdian text on the back identifies the fabric as *zandanichi*, meaning "from the town of Zandana." This same town near Bukhara was still producing fine textiles in the tenth/fourth century, but the word *zandaniji* by then signified cotton rather than silk. A local historian of Bukhara tells us how widespread the trade in this fabric was:

> The specialty of the place is *Zandaniji*, which is a kind of [cotton] cloth (*karbas*) made in Zandana. It is a fine cloth and is made in large quantities. Much of that cloth is woven in other villages of Bukhara, but it is also called *Zandaniji* because it first appeared in this village. That cloth is exported to all countries such as Iraq, Fars, Kirman, Hindustan and elsewhere. All of the nobles and rulers make garments of it, and they buy it at the same price as [silk] brocade (*diba*).[25]

Continuing this impressionistic narrative into the tenth/fourth century will take us beyond the quantifiable data that has so far been presented, but it will set the stage for the discussion of climate change in the next two chapters. Two developments are of particular significance.

First, as has already been mentioned, the tax rates for wheat and barley plummeted between the beginning and the end of the ninth/third century, at least in the districts of Qom and Hamadan. Since there is nothing to indicate that the total Iranian population grew substantially during the first century and a half of Muslim rule, which was marked by repeated military campaigns and extensive social and economic dislocation, the combination of cotton and conversion must have drawn down the rural workforce engaged in food production. At the same time, from the mid-ninth/third through the early tenth/fourth century, urbanization dramatically increased. Whatever the complex of factors that contributed to urban growth (conversion to Islam and the manufacture and export of cotton were certainly two), migration from the countryside must have become a further drain on the agricultural workforce. It seems likely, therefore, that the reduction in the tax rate for wheat and barley reflects a growing realization in the tenth/fourth century that certain heavily urbanized districts of Iran were running out of food.

Second, as the number of Iranians and Iraqis not yet converted grew smaller and smaller in the tenth/fourth century, the cotton industry became less exuberant. Moreover, the Sasanid-era clothing aesthetic began to return. Late converts had more conservative tastes and were more likely to come from the old land-holding class of *dihqans* and their dependents, which might reasonably be supposed to favor the old Sasanid aesthetic. The heyday of the Arabs in Iranian society had come to an end, and dressing like an Arab no longer had the appeal it once had. Stark white pottery decorated with ornamental Arabic characters, but never containing words in the Persian language, faded out as buff ware featuring hunting and feasting scenes derived from Sasanid silverwork rose in popularity. Imported silk, and silk produced locally in regions like Gorgan, regained its cachet (at the highest social levels it had never truly lost it), leaving plain white gowns as the garb of the ulama and *karbas* shrouds as the garb of the dead.

# Chapter Three
## THE BIG CHILL

I N HIS BOOK *THE TURKS IN WORLD HISTORY*, Carter Findley outlines the geographical features of the Turco-Mongolian steppe lands and then makes the following wise comment: "Only a few short, foolish steps lie between describing these environments and advancing environmentally determinist arguments about them."[1] As we turn to the topic of climatic change, we shall see how far we can advance in the direction he warns against.

My thesis will be that Iran experienced a significant cold spell in the first half of the tenth/fourth century, followed by prolonged climatic cooling in the eleventh/fifth and early twelfth/sixth centuries. The colder weather affected not just Iran, but Central Asia, Mesopotamia as far south as Baghdad, Anatolia, and Russia. First will come the evidence for this climate shift. Then we shall advance cautiously down the deterministic road by exploring both the more speculative and the more certain effects of the apparent cooling. The more speculative argument will correlate the hypothesized Big Chill with a general agricultural and demographic decline in the northern districts of the Iranian plateau that included the effective end of the cotton boom. What renders this speculative is a lack of a consistent correlation of scientific evidence with climatic events in places that may also have been affected, such as northern China, and a shortage, though not a total absence, of strong anecdotal evidence corresponding to what should have been the coldest years at the turn of the twelfth/sixth century.

As for the more certain impact of the cold, this involves the folk migration into northeastern Iran of the Oghuz Turks, known in Arabic as the

Ghuzz and usually described in the sources of the period as Turkomans. The textual, geographic, and biological data associated with the first two episodes of tribal relocation in the first half of the eleventh/fifth century, and their correspondence with anecdotal evidence of bad weather, correlates too closely with the strictly scientific evidence to be considered mere happenstance.

At the end of January in 926/313 heavy snow fell in Baghdad. Before this day there were six days of intense cold. Then after the snowfall the cold became even sharper, exceeding all bounds to the extent that most of the date palms in Baghdad and its environs perished, and the fig and citrus trees withered and died. Wine, rosewater, and vinegar froze. The banks of the Tigris iced up at Baghdad, and most of the Euphrates froze at Anbar [at the same latitude as Baghdad]. At Mosul [200 miles to the north] the Tigris froze completely so that pack animals crossed it. A *hadith* reciter named Abu Zikra assembled a class on the ice in the middle of the river, and they took dictation from him. Then the cold broke with wind from the south and heavy rain.[2]

On November 24, 1007/398 snow fell in Baghdad. It accumulated to one *dhira'* in one place and to one-and-a-half *dhira'* in another. [A *dhira'* is a unit of length equal to the average distance from elbows to fingertips.] It stayed on the ground for two weeks without melting. People shoveled it from their roofs into the streets and lanes. Then it began to melt, but traces of it remained in some places for almost twenty days. The snowfall extended to Tikrit [80 miles to the north], and letters arrived from Wasit [100 miles to the south] mentioning the fall there between Batiha and Basra, Kufa, Abadan, and Mahruban.[3]

So reports the twelfth-/sixth-century man of religion Ibn al-Jawzi (d. 1200/596) in his Baghdad-based chronicle *Al-Muntazam fi Ta'rikh al-Muluk wa'l-Umam*, the published portion of which begins in the year 871/257. These snowfalls were eighty years apart, but they were not unique occurrences. Ibn al-Jawzi's descriptions of less vivid episodes of winter cold will be detailed later in this chapter. Yet only one of his severe-cold stories dates to the half century preceding the year 920/308. For that date he relates the following:

"In July of this year, the air got so cold that people came down from their roofs and wrapped themselves in blankets. Then during the winter severe cold damaged the dates and trees, and a lot of snow fell."[6] The closest Ibn al-Jawzi comes to reporting severe winter weather before that year is in a report for January 904/291, when snow fell on one day from noon until evening.[7] In other words, during the half century covered by the chronicle prior to the frigid winter of 920/308, and presumably for many decades before that, severe winter cold was so uncommon in Baghdad that a five-hour snow shower in January was big enough news to be preserved in historical memory.

Today a five-hour snow shower in Baghdad would be as startling and memorable as it was in 904/291. As for a November blizzard blanketing the city with two feet of snow and staying on the ground for more than two weeks, as is reported for 1007/398, it would be meteorologically inconceivable. Modern weather data covering every month from 1888 to 1980 show the twenty-four-hour average temperature of Baghdad in the month of November to be 63 degrees Fahrenheit. The average for December is 52 degrees. January, the coldest month of the year, has a twenty-four-hour average temperature of 49 degrees. These averages, which take into account both the high and low temperatures of the day, show that a significant and long-lasting snowfall in Baghdad is a virtual impossibility in today's climate. Even if some snow did fall during a cold night, it would melt the next morning; and the orange and fig trees that died in 926/313 would survive the brief chill.

The cautious historian must take into account, of course, the possibility that Ibn al-Jawzi's reports are mere historiographical artifacts. He reported these weather events in the late twelfth/sixth century, more than 200 years after they supposedly occurred. So he clearly depended on earlier writers whose works are no longer extant. Do his bad-weather stories accurately reflect the severity of the events? Does he include every freeze and snowfall mentioned in his sources? We have no way of knowing. Does he use bad-weather reports for symbolic purposes, such as to hint at a correlation between meteorological anomalies and times of worldly turmoil and hazard? Probably not. His bad-weather years do not coincide in any obvious way with either political or religious calamities. Moreover, his reports, albeit secondhand, have the flavor of what must originally have been firsthand observation. The specification of which fluids froze, which he includes in more than one report, is particularly telling, because it reflects an awareness of freezing temperature differences in an era before thermometers. Today vinegar typically freezes at 28 degrees Fahrenheit and wine at 15 degrees. The freezing point of rosewater is more variable, as is that of animal urine, which varies, like saltwater, with the quantity of dissolved impurities.

Baghdad residents of Ibn al-Jawzi's own time probably read his blizzard reports with the same sort of puzzlement that such reports elicit today, for the Big Chill that we shall be describing was certainly over by the middle of the twelfth/sixth century. Comparative evidence to this effect comes from the historian Ibn al-Fuwati (d. 1323/723), who compiled a Baghdad-based chronicle covering the years 1228–1299/625–698. His work provides an opportunity to test the quality of Ibn al-Jawzi's reports. Over seventy years, Ibn al-Fuwati reports eight unusual floods on the Tigris or Euphrates rivers.[8] This puts his observations of important natural phenomena (nothing imperiled the river city of Baghdad so much as a disastrous flood) on a par with Ibn al-Jawzi, who mentions unusual floods approximately five times in every fifty years over the substantially longer period that his chronicle covers. Yet Ibn al-Fuwati mentions only one winter with freezing weather and has no tales to tell about great blizzards or people crossing the frozen Tigris on horseback.

Of course, weather stories haphazardly preserved in chronicles do not constitute a trend. What is needed to link such reports into a pattern of climatic change is a context in which to place both the deep freeze of 926/313 and the blizzard of 1007/398. Field research completed in 1999/1419 by a team from the Tree-Ring Laboratory at the Lamont-Doherty Earth Observatory of Columbia University provides that context.[9] An analysis of tree-ring thicknesses from Solongotyn Davaa in western Mongolia, as shown on figure 3.1, indicates that the Iranian cotton boom described in the preceding chapters occurred during a period of notable warmth, except for a cold period between roughly 920/307 and 943/331. Then, at the beginning of the eleventh/fifth century, temperatures dropped significantly, reaching a consistent low level by century's end. The cold then continued well into the twelfth/sixth century. Though the Lamont-Doherty researchers classify these data as statistically robust, their report has one apparent deficiency: western Mongolia is a long way from Iran.

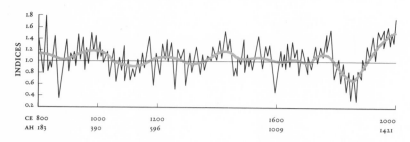

FIGURE 3.1.    Graph of tree-ring variation from Solongotyn Davaa, Mongolia. (After
Rosanne D'Arrigo, Gordon Jacoby, et al., "1738 Years of Mongolian Tempera-
ture Variability Inferred from a Tree-Ring Width Chronology of Siberian Pine,"
*Geophysical Research Letters,* vol. 28, no. 3, p. 544.)

What links these Mongolian tree rings to the winter weather of Iran is
the meteorological phenomenon known as the Siberian High, a massive,
clockwise-rotating, vortex (anticyclone) of high-pressure air that forms every
winter north of the lofty mountain ranges ringing Tibet. As figure 3.2 illus-
trates, the Siberian High affects Eurasian winter weather all the way from
northern China to Russia, though the effect can differ from one region to
another because of encounters with other weather systems. In the Middle
East, the Siberian High introduces cold air into northern Iran, Mesopotamia,
and Anatolia. This regime not only can produce heavy winter snows when it
contacts moist westerly winds from the Mediterranean, but can also block
those winds and thus generate drought conditions along with severe cold.

Since the possibility of a lasting shift to a colder weather regime in the
northern Middle East has not previously been discussed for this time period
in the literature on climate history, it is necessary to ask how it relates to the
generally accepted outlines of that history. The contemporary debate over
global warming has attracted attention to evidence of climatic fluctuations
in earlier times, but it has also biased that attention toward reconstructions
of climate on a global or at least hemispheric scale, as opposed to more localized episodes. The unprecedented warming trend of the past hundred and
fifty years has been compared to an earlier phenomenon that climate historians have labeled the Medieval Warm Period. This period was initially hypothesized on the basis of European data. Starting as early as the ninth/third
century, depending on whose analysis you follow, the Medieval Warm Period
is thought to have extended through the thirteenth/seventh century, after

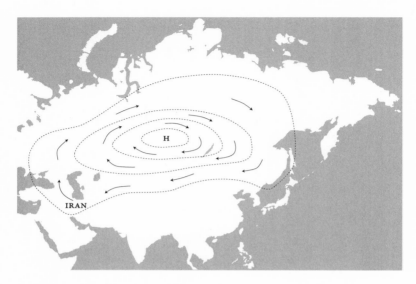

FIGURE 3.2.    Map of Asia showing Siberian High.

which the climate slowly worsened, eventually giving rise to the Little Ice Age. Various dates are assigned to this cooling trend; it was certainly well under way by 1600/1008,[10] but no climate historian pushes it back as far as that snowy Baghdad November of 1007/398.

The questions climate historians ask go beyond establishing local weather facts. Given the globally interconnected character of certain weather cycles, they want to know how broadly the effects of the Medieval Warm Period and Little Ice Age were felt. If they could be conclusively shown to be global, or even hemisphere-wide, such a finding would bear on the general hypothesis that human activities have a recurrent history of affecting world climate. The search for such broad interconnections has led climatologists to combine and weigh data of many different sorts from many different areas, and this has introduced complexity into what began as local, and seemingly clear-cut, historical indications of warmer times giving way to colder times, and vice versa.

Our approach here departs from this analytical trend. It is local, at least in comparison with hemisphere-wide projections, and it concerns a single weather system, the Siberian High, and its effect on the northern Middle East. It also relies on a single scientific indicator, Mongolian tree rings. Yet the broad Medieval Warm Period hypothesis remains important for us because our proposal that there was a century of persistent cold winters in at least some regions affected by the Siberian High system apparently contradicts it.[11] In Europe, evidence for a Medieval Warm Period is diverse and persuasive. Purely scientific indicators aside, ordinary historians put great store in textual evidence of Viking settlement in Iceland and Newfoundland, monastic wine production in England, and the expansion of grain farming in Estonia.[12] What has come into question with the accumulation of data from other parts of the world, and with an ever-greater diversity and sophistication of scientific indicators, has been how widespread this European warm period was. According to the 2001 report of the United Nations Intergovernmental Panel on Climate Change:

> current evidence does not support globally synchronous periods of anomalous cold or warmth over this timeframe, and the conventional terms of "Little Ice Age" and "Medieval Warm Period" appear to have limited utility in describing trends in hemispheric or global mean temperature changes in past centuries.... As with the "Little Ice Age," the posited "Medieval Warm Period" appears to have been less distinct, more moderate in amplitude, and somewhat different in timing at the hemispheric scale than is typically inferred for the conventionally-defined European epoch.[13]

Willie Soon and Sallie Baliunas, in their exhaustive reappraisal of the debate published in 2003, express similar caution but reach a less negative conclusion: "The picture emerges from many localities that both the Little Ice Age and Medieval Warm Period are widespread and perhaps *not precisely timed or synchronous* phenomena.... Our many local answers confirm that both the Medieval Climatic Anomaly and the Little Ice Age Climatic Anomaly are worthy of their respective labels" (emphasis added).[14]

Given the reservations that have accumulated as more and more data have been analyzed, the question is whether this highly technical debate should frame our examination of weather data from early Islamic Iran. On the one hand, if the Medieval Warm Period did indeed constitute a consistent hemispheric phenomenon, the Baghdad hard freeze of 926/313 and blizzard of 1007/398 would be situated in the very heart of what should have been an era of record balminess. Ibn al-Jawzi's reports would thus constitute an anomaly every bit as striking as the warm climate of Viking Iceland appeared to be to the historians who first called attention to it. Indeed, if historians of medieval Baghdad had been the first to arrive on the field of climatic battle, they might well have postulated a Medieval Cold Period. On the other hand, the scientific finding that the Medieval Warm Period may not be a "precisely timed or synchronous phenomen[on]" and that it "appears to have been less distinct, more moderate in amplitude, and somewhat different in timing at the hemispheric scale than is typically inferred for the conventionally defined European epoch" may provide the leeway for focusing exclusively on Iran, Mesopotamia, and Anatolia and putting on hold the question of how the experience of these areas compares with the undisputed warmth of northern Europe in the tenth/fourth through twelfth/sixth centuries.

A second set of Mongolian tree rings provides an example of how general climate indices can obscure more localized weather fluctuations. The tree rings in this case come from Tarvagatay, a Mongolian mountain pass not far from Solongotyin Davaa. The Tarvagatay sequence covers only 450 years instead of the 1700-year span of the Solongotyin Davaa data, but a published study compares the data for those years with a generalized temperature reconstruction for the Northern Hemisphere based on a wide variety of indicators, precisely the kind of combined climate appraisal that has raised questions about the timing and extent of the Medieval Warm Period and the Little Ice age.[15] For the early 1870s/late 1280s, both the Tarvagatay and the Solongotyin Davaa data indicate a sudden dip into near-record coldness. However, the multicomponent generalized Northern Hemisphere curve shows stable temperatures in the cool range from 1850/1266 until around 1890/1307. As historians of Russia, Iran, and the Ottoman Empire will recall, the 1870s were severe famine years over a broad region affected by the Siberian High.[16] Here is a case, then, where the Mongolian tree-ring data fit the weather actually experienced in the region we are concerned with far better than the hypothesized hemisphere-wide indicator.

Although one must exercise caution in making inferences from two- or three-year anomalies, they should not be ignored.[17] An instructive example comes from the year 855/241, when Solongotyin data not shown in figure 3.1 show another cold spike of near record dimension squeezed in the middle of a series of much warmer years. Since Ibn al-Jawzi's chronicle does not begin

until 871/257, the timeline of Baghdad weather that we have been using includes no information on this earlier year. However, another chronicler,
Hamza al-Isfahani, whose work was completed in 961/349, fills in the gap:

> In the year 855/241 a freezing cold wind emerged from the land of the
> Turks [Central Asia] and moved toward Sarakhs [in Khurasan]. Many
> people got a severe chill. Unable to resist the cold, coughing, and pain,
> they died. The wind then shifted from Sarakhs to Nishapur and reached
> the city of Rayy [modern Tehran]. Then this cold wind moved and blew
> to Hamadan and Holvan [in western Iran]. The wind was divided into
> two branches. One branch of wind moved to the right in the direction
> of the city of Samarra [on the Tigris north of Baghdad], and the other
> branch of severe cold wind reached the city of Baghdad. Many people
> were affected by it and died. Finally the wind reached the city of Basra [at
> the head of the Persian Gulf] and ended in Ahwaz. [18]

Two year-specific correlations (855/241 and 1870–4/1286–90) between
extreme cold signaled by Mongolian tree rings and severe cold or famine in
the northern Middle East do not prove that the Solongotyin Davaa data always reflect the weather experienced in the western reaches of the region affected by the Siberian High. But they encourage one to think that the longer
trends covering the ninth/third through twelfth/sixth centuries may well
provide a reliable guide. Ideally, this conclusion would now be buttressed by
a learned digression about how temperatures are inferred from the widths of
tree rings and how fluctuations in the intensity and westward extension of
the Siberian High relate to another climatic phenomenon called the North
Atlantic Oscillation. Alas, the reader will have to turn elsewhere for this degree of scientific expertise on an extremely complex topic.[19]
   Although the Mongolian tree-ring series sets the chronological parame-
ters of the cold period we are concerned with here, textual descriptions better
reflect the reality people lived through. Baghdad must have been on the
fringe of the affected region, but the comments of its chronicler Ibn al-Jawzi
provide our best source on unusual weather. Striking stories come from the
decades following the blizzard of 1007/398, when the tree rings indicate that
winters were becoming increasingly cold:

1027/417

In this year, continuously from November to January, came a cold that no one had ever known before. Water froze solid throughout this period, including the shores of the Tigris and the wide canals. As for the water wheels and smaller channels, they were frozen solid. People suffered from this severity, and many were prevented from doing things and moving about.[20]

1028/418

In April large hail struck the districts of Qatrabbul, al-Nu'maniyya, and al-Nil and affected the crops in these areas. It killed many wild and domestic animals, and it was reported that one hailstone weighed two *ratls* or more [approximately two pounds]. . . . In November a cold wind blew from the west, and the cold lasted until the beginning of January. It went beyond normal. The banks of the Tigris froze along with vinegar, date wine, and the urine of animals. I saw a waterwheel that had stopped because of the frozen water, which had become like pillars in its holes.[21]

1029/419

We mentioned what happened to the dates last year because of cold and wind. So this year there was a dearth of animal feed, except for what was imported. It cost one *jalali dinar* [a gold coin] for every three *ratls* [approximately three pounds]. The cold became so intense that the shores of the Tigris froze, and the Bedouin stopped at 'Ukbara from making their migrations because of the freezing in the vicinity. Tens of thousands of date palms died in Baghdad.[22]

So much for Baghdad; our concern is Iran. If the severe winters reported for Baghdad derive from the Siberian High spreading a deep chill all the way from Mongolia, then there should be some parallel stories of intense cold from Iran. Here, however, we run into two complications. First, chronicles for Iran in this period are few and far between. And second, the climate of northern Iran, unlike that of Baghdad, is conventionally described in terms of "continental extremes"; that is, hot summers and cold winters. So the contrast between a normally cold winter and a truly frigid winter might not have been so evident, or so historically memorable, as a blizzard along the banks of the Tigris. Nevertheless, a detailed travel account by a wayfarer from Baghdad and certain passages in Hamza al-Isfahani's tenth-/fourth-century chronicle and Abu al-Fazl Bayhaqi's history of the third decade of the eleventh/fifth century parallel the dire reports of Ibn al-Jawzi.

Ahmad ibn Fadlan, the wayfarer, served as the secretary of an embassy sent by the Caliph al-Muqtadir to the king of the Turkish Bulgars then living on the lower reaches of the Volga River north of the Caspian Sea.[23] The embassy departed from Baghdad in July 921/309, just a few months after the end of the capital's first frigid winter as reported by Ibn al-Jawzi. It made its way through the Zagros Mountains and across northern Iran following the main route of the Silk Road all the way to Bukhara. From there, warned about the harshness of winter, it doubled back to the Oxus River (modern Amu Darya) and proceeded northward by boat toward the Aral Sea, or more properly, toward the flourishing farmlands of Khwarazm, the desert-framed region formed by the delta of the Oxus, where it entered the sea. There the embassy remained for four months, November through February, prevented from going further by the severity of the winter cold. For three of those months the river froze solid enough "from end to end" for horses, mules, and carts to travel on it as if it were a highway.[24]

Ibn Fadlan reports from that period an anecdote that will reenter our discussion in a different context in the next chapter. It seems that two men took twelve camels out to collect wood in some brushy swamps, but somehow they forgot to bring any implements for starting a fire. When they awoke after spending the night in the cold, they found that all the camels had frozen to death. Returning to his own personal observations, he remarks: "I saw weather where the cold made the market and streets so empty that a person could walk around without seeing or encountering a single soul. I used to come out of the public bath, and when I entered a house, I would notice that my beard was a single block of ice until I held it near the fire."[25] In March, the embassy set off again after buying some "Turkish camels." Yet they still encountered snow that reached up to their camels' knees and cold so severe as to make them forget the cold they had already endured during their stay in Khwarazm.[26]

Coming from Baghdad, Ibn Fadlan may not have been able to state explicitly that the cold he experienced in Khwarazm, which is today in Uzbekistan, was unprecedented, but the tenor of his account certainly implies this, particularly his reports of streets and markets being entirely empty as if even the local population had no familiarity with such severe weather. For comparison, the current minimum temperatures for Nukus, which is today the main city of the historic province of Khwarazm, are 30.7 degrees in November, when Ibn Fadlan's embassy arrived, and 30.6 degrees in March, when it departed. The highs for these months are 50.4 and 51.1, respectively.

If Ibn Fadlan's account marks the beginning of the tenth-/fourth-century cold spell, Hamza al-Isfahani describes the weather toward its end: "In the year 942/330 on the twentieth day of the month of Aban [mid-autumn] an unprecedented snow fell on the city [Isfahan]."[27]

In the early morning of Nowruz [the vernal equinox] in the year 943/332, when the residents of Isfahan woke up they witnessed a tremendous snowfall that had covered the whole city. The amount of snow was so great that people were not able to move around. We never had snow in the springtime. Following the snow a severe cold wind began to blow, and people started their Nowruz while all the trees were badly damaged. This wind that caused a lot of damage then shifted toward the eastern parts. The extent of damage was so great that people did not have fruit in that year.[28]

Turning to the more prolonged chill that began at the beginning of the eleventh/end of the fourth century, the historian Bayhaqi relates the following episodes:

1035/426
The Amir left Nishapur on Sunday 12 Rabi' I [25 January 1035] and took the Esfarayen road to Gorgan. It felt bitterly cold on the way, with very strong winds, especially up to the head of the Dinar-e Sari valley. We were traveling in the last month of winter and I, Bu'l-Fazl, was feeling so bitterly cold while riding my horse that when we reached the head of the valley I felt as if I was not wearing anything at all, in spite of the fact that I had taken all precautions and was wearing quilted trousers stuffed with feathers and a jacket of red fox fur and had donned a rainproof coat.[29]

This might be dismissed as normal hyperbole but for the fact that in October of the same year, Bayhaqi describes a defeated Turkish army fleeing across the frozen Oxus River. On this the noted Russian orientalist Wilhelm Barthold commented: "This story evokes some doubt; it is strange that as early as October a whole army could cross the Amu-Darya on ice."[30] However, the date is entirely compatible with the account already cited from Ibn Fadlan.

### 1037/429

During the whole time I was in the service of this great dynasty, I never witnessed a winter at Ghaznin [south of Kabul in Afghanistan] as hard as that of this year.[31]

### 1038/430

The Amir set out from Balkh [northern Afghanistan] heading for Termez [across the Oxus River in Tajikistan] on Monday, the nineteenth of this month [19 December 1038]. He crossed by the bridge and encamped on the plain facing the fortress of Termez. My master accompanied the Amir on this journey, and I went with him. It was bitterly cold, colder than anyone could remember in their lifetime. . . . The cold there was of another degree of intensity, and snow fell continuously. The army suffered more on this expedition than on any other.[32]

Other reports focus on crop failure and famine. The following notice in Bayhaqi from January of 1040/431 reflects the food situation following the frigid winter just mentioned:

### 1040/431

Nishapur was not the city I knew from the past: it now lay in ruins with only vestiges of habitation and urban life. A *man* (maund) of bread sold for three dirhams. Property owners (*kadkhodayan*) had torn off the roofs of their houses and sold them. A great number of people, together with their families and children, had died from hunger. The price of landed property had plummeted . . . the weather was bitterly cold and life was becoming hard to bear. Such a famine in Nishapur could not be recalled, and large numbers of people died, soldiers and civilians alike. . . . After we went back, a *man* of bread had become thirteen dirhams at Nishapur, and the greater part of the population of the city and its outlying regions died. . . . The position regarding food and fodder got so serious that camels were led as far as Damghan, and food and fodder brought back from there. It goes without saying that the Turkmens did not harass or hover around us, since they too were taken up with their own welfare, since this dearth and famine had spread everywhere. [33]

Damghan was 250 miles from Nishapur, which indicates that crop failures affected all Khurasan. Bayhaqi picks up the story again at the time of Nowruz, the vernal equinox:

The Amir had pitched his tent on an eminence, and the army had encamped in battle formation, fully equipped. He was drinking wine, and was not going out in person with the main body of the army to confront the enemy but was waiting for the supplies of grain to arrive. The prices had spiraled up to such an extent that a *man* of bread went up to thirteen dirhams, but was still scarce, and as for barley, it was nowhere to be found. They ransacked Tus [40 miles east of Nishapur] and its surroundings, and whoever had even a *man* of corn was forced to part with it. . . . Many people and livestock perished from lack of food and fodder, for it is obvious how long one can survive on a diet of rough weeds and bramble.[34]

By May the new crop of winter wheat and barley should have been nearing harvest, but the famine continued:

The Amir departed from there, heading towards Sarakhs [on the Iran-Turkmenistan border], on Saturday, 19 Shaʿban [5 May]. Before we could reach Sarakhs, countless horses dropped dead on the road, and the men were all immersed in deep despair from hunger and dearth of food. We reached there on 28 Shaʿban [14 May]. The town looked parched and in ruins, and there was not a single shoot of corn anywhere. The inhabitants had all fled, and the plains and mountains looked scorched, with not a speck of vegetation in sight. The troops were dumbfounded. They would go and fetch from afar bits of rotten vegetation that rainwater had washed up and deposited in the surrounding plains in former times, and they would sprinkle water on them and throw them before their mounts. The beasts would try a mouthful or two but would then lift up their heads and just stare until they died from hunger. The infantry were in no better state.[35]

The relative contributions of cold weather and drought to these two years of crop failure cannot be determined, but these were not the only famine years during the period of bad winters. In 1036/428, just three years earlier, Ibn Funduq, the local historian of the Bayhaq district just west of Nishapur, tells of a famine that necessitated the importation of food from Gorgan, a much warmer district near the Caspian coast.[36] He also reports that for the next seven years, from 1037/429 onward, there were food shortages caused by a cessation of planting and harvesting outside the walled areas of the community. Ibn Funduq's phrasing might lead the reader to surmise that rural insecurity was the central problem in this prolonged period of meager harvests, but Abu al-Fazl Bayhaqi's detailed descriptions of cold winters and general Khurasani crop failure already cited for the years 1037–1040/429–431 clearly link the situation in the town of Bayhaq to the broader agricultural catastrophe.

A slightly earlier famine in the same region received an excessively florid account in the *Kitab-i Yamini* of Abu Nasr Muhammad al-ʿUtbi:

In the year 1011/401, in the province of Khurasan, generally, and in the city of Nishapur, particularly, a wide-spread famine, and a frightful and calamitous scarcity occurred. . . . Such was the extent of the calamity that, in the district of Nishapur, nearly 100,000 men perished, and no one was at liberty to wash, coffin, or inter them, but placed them in the ground in the clothes they had. . . . Some arrested their last breath by means of grass and hay, until all sustenance from sown fields and cultivated things were [sic] cut off. . . . And the Sultan during those days commanded, and sent an edict into the provinces of the kingdom, ordaining that the revenue officers and magistrates should empty the granaries of corn, and distribute amongst the poor and wretched. . . . And that year came to an end in the same state, until the produce of the year 1012/402 arrived, when the fire of that calamity was extinguished, and that extremity was remedied.[37]

Like the weather reports from Baghdad, these chance mentions of cold winters and famines in Khurasan cannot be sewn together into a seamless narrative of climatic change. (We experience the same uncertainty today when a chilly spring following a balmy winter casts doubt on the reality of global warming—until we look at the scientific data.) But the temperature curve derived from the Mongolian tree rings so closely reflects the dating of these weather events that one may cautiously advance the following conclusions:

1. The northern Middle East away from the Mediterranean (i.e., northern Iran, Mesopotamia from Baghdad north, and eastern Anatolia) experienced comparatively warm winters throughout the ninth/third and tenth/fourth centuries, with the exception of a sharp cold period from 920/308 to 943/331.

2. A deeper chill set in early in the eleventh/fifth century and lasted well into the twelfth/sixth century.

3. Serious famines recurred frequently during at least the early part of this cold period.

A search for bad-weather stories from the later decades of the Big Chill, 1050–1130/441–524, has turned up relatively few, even though the tree-ring analysis points to continuing cold. But those that do appear bespeak the grinding impact of stress in the agricultural economy. The historian Ibn al-Athir (1160–1233/554–630) deals broadly with the political history of the entire Islamic world in his work *al-Kamil fi'l-Ta'rikh* and rarely touchs on minor concerns like weather. Yet for the year 1098/492 he reports: "In Khurasan, there was a sharp increase in prices, with food prices becoming impossible. It lasted for two years. The reason was cold weather that entirely destroyed the crops. Afterward the people were visited by pestilential disease. A large number of them died, making it impossible to bury them all."[38] In the following year, he reports: "Prices in Iraq became unstable. A large measure (*kurr*) of wheat reached 70 dinars, or even a good deal more at some moments. The rains didn't come, and the rivers dried up. [Winter is the rainy season in Iraq and in Anatolia, where springtime snowmelt normally causes the Tigris and Euphrates to flood.] So many people died that it was impossible to bury them all."[39]

A different sort of testimony comes in a letter written in the year 1106/500 by the famous theologian al-Ghazali to the Seljuq ruler, Sultan Sanjar: "Be merciful to the people of Tus [al-Ghazali's hometown near Nishapur in Khurasan], who have suffered boundless injustice, whose grain was destroyed by cold and drought, and whose hundred year old trees dried up at the roots. . . . For if you demand something from them, they will all flee and die in the mountains."[40] The closing sentence of this letter is particularly suggestive of the way in which inept government responses to hard times could drive villagers from the land and thus compound the disaster.

Why are there fewer reports of frigid temperatures, drought, crop failure, and famine after 1050/441 than before? The worst-case possibility from the perspective of the argument being made in this book would be that the Mongolian tree-ring data only sporadically reflect the weather of the northern Middle East and should not be given credence without specific textual corroboration. Yet it is precisely in the later decades that the lowest temperatures are indicated, and this is also the point when cold weather hits China as well (see note 9). But there are other possibilities. Relying as he did on what he found in earlier writings, Ibn al-Jawzi may have come to the end of a chronicle that made frequent mention of weather phenomena and moved on to another chronicle that was less attentive to such things. Another alternative is that because weather events are best remembered when they are contrary to expectation, once people became accustomed to chillier winters, they were less inclined to mention specific instances of extreme cold or heavy snow.

A more dire interpretation would take note of the fact that the chronicles covering the period of the chill increasingly relate instances of nomadic depredations, urban factional conflict, rural insecurity, and, in the latest decades, internecine warfare among members of the Seljuq family. If these events were in some measure negative consequences of the climate change, then the weather particulars in and of themselves might have become less noteworthy. In 920 or 1007 extraordinary freezes and snowfalls were big news. But as time passed, the crop failures, famines, and political disorder brought on by the Big Chill claimed the headlines. Iran went through bad times during this period. Agricultural land fell out of production (al-Ghazali's letter to Sultan Sanjar suggests one reason why) and pastoral nomadism occupied more and more territory. Cities that had already been approaching the

limit of the land's ability to feed unproductive urban workers shrank, particularly in northern districts, and the educated elite emigrated to Central Asia,
India, Anatolia, or the Arab lands.[41] A heightened competition for dwindling
resources, particularly in the cities, contributed to all kinds of social disorder,
from lethal factional feuding between Sunni law schools to the rise of a violent sort of Isma'ili Shi'ite sectarianism. However, in exploring these consequences of the Big Chill, we should look at how cotton farming in particular
weathered the transition from warm to cold winters.

The Big Chill signaled by the Mongolian tree-ring data roughly coincides
with a pronounced decline in Iran's cotton industry. Cotton did not reappear as a fiber of major economic importance until early modern times, when
printed fabrics inspired by Indian techniques became popular, and raw cotton from northern Iran began to be exported in large quantities to Russia,
primarily in the nineteenth/thirteenth century.[42] This does not mean that
cotton made no return after the Big Chill. When it did, however, it was
grown more in southern than in northern Iran, and its economic role was
local rather than transregional.

André Miquel, in the first volume of his monumental *La géographie humaine du monde musulman jusqu'au milieu du $11^e$ siècle,* which encompasses
all parts of the Islamic world, lists the references to cotton growing and cotton export that he found in four major works of Arabic geography completed
before the year 1000/390 (i.e., before the Big Chill).[43] Half—twenty-one out
of forty-one—pertain to the Iran-Afghanistan-Central Asia region, and
two-thirds of those refer specifically to cities or provinces north of Isfahan.
Miquel's tabulation can be compared with a later geographical work penned
by a government official named Hamd-Allah Mustawfi in 1340/740, when
the Big Chill had faded from memory.[44] Mustawfi mentions only twelve Iranian cotton-producing areas, and of those twelve, all but three are located
either in southern Iran or in the balmy Caspian lowlands. More important,
the locales he mentions are mostly villages, not cities, which indicates local
consumption rather than a major export trade in cotton textiles. Major cities
like Isfahan, Qazvin, Nishapur, Marv, Bukhara, Samarqand, and Rayy that

had dominated the cotton industry prior to the year 1000/390 are no longer mentioned as producing areas. Moreover, these cities are not named as cotton centers in Ruy Gonzalez de Clavijo's narrative of an embassy to the court of Timur in the years 1403–1406/805–808.[45] His observations on cottons imported to Sultaniyeh, Timur's capital in northwestern Iran, specify Shiraz, Yazd, and Khurasan as producing areas: two southern cities and one general northeastern province.

The southward shift in cotton growing hints at climate change having lingering effects. However, it is hard to determine whether cold weather in and of itself brought devastation to the cotton planters of the north. Fluctuations in the Siberian High, a winter phenomenon, probably did not diminish the heat of summer or shorten the growing season to less than the five months needed for cotton plants to mature. To be sure, the cotton plant is sensitive to cold, but the greatest sensitivity is at the time of planting. Seeds do not germinate properly if the soil temperature falls below 65 degrees Fahrenheit. Without thermometers, Iran's cotton farmers may well have occasionally sown their crops too early after a severe winter. An agricultural almanac from Yemen, where Iran's cotton culture probably originated, matches crop activities to specific times of year, suggesting that farmers relied more on time-honored tradition than on technical calculation in determining the best date for planting.[46] However, as experienced men of the soil, Iran's cotton farmers probably learned from these mistakes and by trial and error adapted their practices to the chillier temperatures.

The greater impact of the cold, and the one signaled by the famine reports, must have been on winter crops, notably the staple grains that sustained both man and beast.[47] The plummeting rate of taxation on wheat and barley discussed in the previous chapter indicates that pressure on food resources had already begun by the beginning of the tenth/fourth century, in apparent response to the exuberant urban growth and rural–urban migration of that period.[48] If this analysis is sound, then the effect of the Big Chill on cotton may have been more indirect than direct. Reduced harvests caused by cold weather or rural insecurity would have only added to an already existing pressure on farmers to convert cotton fields into wheat fields.

Another factor may also have contributed to lower cotton production: waning prestige as a fabric and loss of the luxury market to silk. The tabulation of occupational names borne by ulama in five different cities (see table 2.1) revealed that the number of cotton growers roughly equaled the number of cotton cloth merchants in four Iranian cities, whereas the ratio in Baghdad was one cotton farmer to every five cotton cloth dealers. Excluded from table 2.1, however, was the occupational information from the most extensive Iranian biographical dictionary dealing specifically with the eleventh/fifth century, ʿAbd al-Ghafir al-Farisi's *Kitab al-Siyaq li Taʾrikh Naisabur*.[49] Al-Farisi's work continued the compilation of al-Hakim al-Naisaburi, whose work *was* used for table 2.1. Like al-Hakim, al-Farisi divided his biographies into chronological categories. His first chronological category contains the biographies of people who died between roughly 1014/405 and 1033/425. These individuals lived most of their lives before the Big Chill set in, so we will set the death-date limits back by twenty years to approximate the time when their occupational epithets may have signified an active involvement with the economy. This makes the boundary dates for Period 1 994–1013/383–403. The limiting dates for Period 2 and Period 3, with the same twenty-year setback, are 1014–1047/404–438 and 1047–1110/439–503, respectively. It is with the individuals included in these two later periods that evidence of a change in the cotton industry becomes apparent.

The decline of the cotton industry as a prestige occupation shows clearly in table 3.1. Roughly one third of the fourth-/tenth-century occupational epithets contained in al-Hakim's compilation relate to cotton growing and the production of cotton cloth. This drops by half, to an average of 15 percent in the three chronological divisions of al-Farisi's work, with the lowest percentage being in Period 3. Decline in the industry as a whole becomes even more striking if we exclude the trade in *karbas*, a sturdy, heavy-duty fabric that seems to have become a Nishapur specialty inasmuch as the name *Karabisi* rarely appears elsewhere in Iran. Without *karbas*, cotton sinks from 25 percent of all epithets to 8 percent, a drop of two thirds. If one looks specifically at cotton growers, the falloff is even greater than two thirds, going from 10 percent in al-Hakim to under 3 percent in al-Farisi.

Though the number totals shown in table 3.1 are all so small as to make percentage calculations precarious, some corroboration of cotton's decline can be gleaned from information about other trades. The leather industry,

TABLE 3.1   Occupational names in Nishapur's cotton industry

| DEATH DATES SET BACK 20 YEARS | COTTON AS A CROP: QATTAN | COTTON CLOTH: BAZZAZ | COTTON CANVAS: KARABISI | TOTAL IN COTTON INDUSTRY | TOTAL ALL TRADE EPITHETS |
|---|---|---|---|---|---|
| AL-HAKIM | | | | | |
| 906–926/293–314 | 5 (10%) | 7 (14%) | 3 (6%) | 15 (30%) | 48 |
| 926–994/314–384 | 8 (10%) | 10 (13%) | 15 (19%) | 33 (42%) | 78 |
| AL-FARISI | | | | | |
| 994–1013/383–403 | 1 (2%) | 2 (4%) | 5 (10%) | 8 (16%) | 49 |
| 1014–1047/404–438 | 3 (3%) | 9 (9%) | 8 (8%) | 20 (20%) | 97 |
| 1047–1110/439–503 | 3 (2%) | 5 (4%) | 8 (5%) | 16 (11%) | 147 |

as portrayed in table 3.2, offers an instructive comparison. The numbers here are so small as to make percentage comparisons truly meaningless, but the overall trend from the fourth/tenth to the fifth/eleventh century is suggestive. The last two time periods of al-Hakim's work and the first time period of al-Farisi's cover the century preceding the migration of large numbers of Turkoman nomads into Khurasan. Over those 110 years, eleven members of Nishapur's religious elite bore names pertaining to the leather industry. However, during the eleventh/fifth century, comprising Period 2 and Period 3 of al-Farisi's work, the number of leather merchants totals twenty, almost double the tenth-/fourth-century rate. It is hard to avoid the suspicion that a growing number of Nishapur's scholar-merchants found profit in marketing the skins produced by the extensive flocks of sheep and goats herded by the nomadic newcomers to their region. And it is similarly plausible that the decline in cotton, whether caused by weather, rural insecurity, or changes in demand, was somewhat counterbalanced by the rise of leather.

Professional names associated with fiber commodities imported along the Silk Road (*Farra'*, meaning "furrier"; *Ibrisimi,* meaning "silk merchant"; and *Labbad,* meaning "felt dealer") similarly indicate a movement away from cotton. One furrier and one silk importer appear in Period 1 of al-Farisi, whereas four of the former and one of the latter show up in Period 2, along

TABLE 3.2    Occupational names in Nishapur's leather industry

| DEATH DATES SET BACK 20 YEARS | SADDLER: SARRAJ | LEATHER DEALER: SIKHTIYANI | SKINS DEALER: SARRAM |
|---|---|---|---|
| AL-HAKIM | | | |
| 906–926/293–314 | 1 | 0 | 1 |
| 926–994/314–384 | 3 | 0 | 2 |
| AL-FARISI | | | |
| 994–1013/383–403 | 2 | 2 | 0 |
| 1014–1047/404–438 | 8 | 0 | 1 |
| 1047–1110/439–503 | 6 | 1 | 4 |

with one felt dealer. Two more silk importers are registered in Period 3. The reappearance of these Silk Road commodities, which are almost totally un-represented among the occupational names of Nishapur's ulama between the middle ninth/third and late tenth/fourth century,[50] suggests a reinvigoration of trans-Asian caravan trade. This matter will be pursued further in the next chapter.

Quantitative indicators, especially those based on small number totals, need to be tested against other sorts of evidence. What other observations might support an argument for cotton losing status or commercial prominence in the eleventh/fifth century? Anecdotes are sometimes helpful. Bayhaqi relates the following story in his chronicle of the year 1031/422:

> The next day, Tuesday, the Grand Vizier came to the court, had an audience with the Amir and then came to the Divan. A prayer rug of turquoise-colored satin brocade had been spread out near his usual prominent place. . . . He sent for an inkstand, which they set down, and also for a quire of paper and a lightweight scroll, of the kind that they bring along and set down for viziers. He set to work and wrote there: *"In the name of God, the Merciful, the Compassionate. Praise be to God the lord of*

*the worlds, and blessings upon His Messenger, the Chosen One, Muham-*
*mad, and all his house. God is my sufficiency, and how excellent a guardian*
*is He! O God, help me to do what You desire and what is pleasing to You,*
*through Your mercy, O most merciful of those who show mercy! Let there be*
*given out to the poor and destitute, by way of thanks to God, the Lord of the*
*Two Worlds, 10,000 dirhams of silver coinage, 10,000 dirhams worth of*
*bread, 5,000 dirhams worth of meat, and 10,000 cubits' lengths of [karbas].*[51]

This story from shortly before the Seljuq takeover makes it clear that cotton is not in short supply, at least in the government storehouses. The Grand
Vizier himself, however, sits on silk brocade, and the cotton he distributes to
the poor is heavy-duty stuff, not fine fabric. *Karbas* is obviously the sort of
cotton that was most available in Nishapur.

Visual evidence is also valuable. In the preceding chapter I proposed that
the growth of the cotton industry in the ninth/third century was stimulated
in part by a desire of the Muslim Arabs and of the non-Arab Iranian converts
to Islam to make themselves visibly distinguishable from non-Muslims in the
public arena. Wearing silk brocade garments by the Sasanid elite was recognized as a non-Muslim practice and consequently prohibited in the *hadith* of
Muhammad that were being assiduously collected and transmitted in Iran.
By the end of the tenth/fourth century, however, silk garments, and silk brocade in particular, no longer stirred strong religious opposition. Thenceforth,
plain white cotton cloth continued to be the preferred garb only of the ulama,
and the military and governing elites felt more and more comfortable with
the Sasanid-style luxury fabrics that they had never truly abandoned.

The evidence for this change in taste is diverse but consistent. With respect to the ulama, the *Adab al-imla' wa'l-istimla'* of 'Abd al-Karim al-
Sam'ani, a work on the etiquette of teaching *hadith* by a Khurasani scholar
who died in 1167/562, is unequivocal. Under the prescriptive heading "Let
[the *hadith* reciter] dress in white garments," he quotes the Messenger of God
as saying about white garments: "Your living bodies wear them, your corpses
are wrapped in them; truly they are the best of your garments."[52]

At a more general level, we may recall the tenth-/fourth-century trend
in Nishapuri pottery mentioned in the preceding chapter, to wit, the flagging popularity of slip-painted ware, the plain white ceramic dishes with

ornate Arabic calligraphy, and the growing popularity of buff ware. Though most specimens of buff ware do not feature human figures, those that do closely mirror the designs on Sasanid gold and silver vessels, the characteristic luxury products of the Iranian aristocracy. During the Seljuq period both styles disappear, being replaced by blue wares of various sorts and by painted wares that take up feasting and warrior themes from their buff ware precursors. The stark Arabic calligraphy on a plain white background has no successor.

The onomastic data from which I projected the course of Iranian conversion to Islam in my 1975 book *Conversion to Islam in the Medieval Period* pointed to the late ninth/third century as the beginning of the climax period (i.e., end of the "late majority" phase) in the growth of Iran's Muslim community (see figure 1.4).[53] I have now been persuaded by the observations of constructive critics that this data base underrepresented rural areas and that the climax period was probably not reached until some time in the tenth/ fourth century. Nevertheless, regardless of its precise chronology, the climax period was still a time when many of those members of the landowning elite who had not become prisoners of war during the original Arab conquests, and subsequently converted to Islam to escape slavery, finally gave in to an unstoppable trend and switched their communal identification from Zoroastrian (or Christian) to Muslim. For these high-status individuals of the Late Majority period, the Muslim clothing style sanctioned by *hadith* may have had little appeal. Just as they enjoyed listening to the pre-Islamic Iranian legends that were being collected into the *Shahnameh* or "Book of Kings" by the end of the tenth/fourth century, they preferred the clothing styles of the Sasanid period, both for apparel and as designs on pottery. With Arab caliphal power supplanted by more localized Iranian political regimes, and the permanence of Islam as the religion of Iran no longer in doubt, they saw little reason to dress like Arabs. Indeed, a desire to distinguish themselves from Arabs may have become as common as the desire to look and act like Arabs had been among the earliest generations of Iranian converts.

The Seljuq period of the eleventh/fifth and twelfth/sixth centuries provides abundant visual evidence—pottery, figurines, miniature paintings—of silk brocade being the preferred clothing fabric of the governing elite. This does not mean, however, that *tiraz* ceased to be made for incorporation into royal presentation garments. Not only do the occupational names Tirazi and Mutarriz continue to appear throughout the eleventh century, but Bayhaqi indicates in his description of arrangements made for a subordinate ruler in the year 1030/421 that embroidering the name of a ruler on *tiraz* had become a formal symbol of political legitimacy:

> [A further condition is] that our brother should act as our deputy, in such a way that our own name is proclaimed first from the pulpits in the towns, and the formal intercessory prayers at the Friday sermon (*khutba*) [are] pronounced in our name at those places and then afterwards in his name. With the minting of dirhams and dinars, and the official embroidery on luxury garments (*tiraz-e jama*), they are likewise to write our name first and then his.[54]

However, the Seljuq pictorial evidence reveals that the *tiraz* embroidery was now worn around the upper arm of a brocade garment, rather than being the sole ornamentation on a length of plain or striped cloth (fig. 3.3). What had once amounted to the government's religious endorsement of the cotton industry had become simply a vehicle for affirming the authority of the ruler.

The following conclusions will help summarize and draw together the various threads of argument presented in this chapter:

1. Because of unusually cold winter temperatures influenced by the Siberian High, Iran's climate suffered a two-decades-long chill starting in 920/307, and then sank into a period of severe winter cold and accompanying drought in the early eleventh/fifth century that seems to have continued into the fourth decade of the twelfth/sixth century.
2. Cotton underwent a decline in production during the cold period of the eleventh/fifth century but had already passed its peak of popularity as a distinctively Muslim clothing fabric by the early tenth/fourth century.
3. Religious scholars dealt more often in leather, fur, felt, and imported Chinese silk, the latter three Silk Road commodities, as their involvement in the

FIGURE 3.3.     Tiraz worn on upper arm in Seljuq period. (By permission of the Metropolitan Museum of Art.)

cotton industry declined. But their own personal clothing preference remained plain white cotton.

4. The cotton industry that revived after the return of warmer temperatures centered primarily in southern Iran, with the northern cities that had been central to the early Islamic cotton boom no longer involved.

In mustering the evidence on which these conclusions are based, we have avoided the question of how the migration of the Turkic people known as the Oghuz (Ghuzz) or Turkomans, and the building of the Seljuq empire on the basis of their manpower, fits into these climatic and economic changes. That will be the topic of the next chapter.

# Chapter Four

## OF TURKS AND CAMELS

T HE BIG CHILL DID NOT BY itself bring the Iranian cotton boom to an end. It was an indirect and contributory factor. With the entry of the Oghuz Turkomans into Iran the question of causation is more complicated. This chapter will present a radical argument consisting of two propositions: First, the particular groups of Oghuz Turkomans that moved into Iran in the early eleventh/fifth century herded livestock that included economically significant numbers of one-humped female camels, which they interbred with selected two-humped males to produce superior animals for Silk Road caravans and military remounts. Second, the Big Chill so threatened the survival of the cold-sensitive one-humped stock, which largely disappear in northern Iran during the Seljuq period, that the breeders had no choice but to move south from the northern edge of Turkmenistan's Karakum desert to the southern edge. According to this hypothesis, climate change played the role of primary cause in this epochal folk migration.

Against this proposition is the conventional line of argument loosely based on scanty reports in historical narratives of the period. This places the primary emphasis on complicated political conflicts in the Turkmenistan–Uzbekistan area. With respect to historical causation, this conventional approach would relegate unusual weather events, which were never previously identified as a major causal factor, to the role of an accompanying circumstance of possibly negligible significance. It would not rule out, however, the possibility that the Big Chill influenced the course of Iranian economic history in other ways during the century of Seljuq rule that followed the entry of the Oghuz into Khurasan.

A critical reader's preference between these two arguments, neither of which is supported by either abundant or absolutely conclusive evidence, is as likely to turn on his or her philosophy of history as on the specifics presented. Some people prefer to understand key historical events as the product of the interplay of conscious human activities and decisions, and accordingly abhor deterministic or mechanistic factors like climate change or epidemic disease. The choice at hand is not quite so stark, however. Historians agree that thousands of nomadic families, together with their multitudinous flocks and herds, suddenly began migrating into northeastern Iran after living for five centuries or more in a more northerly region, roughly between the Caspian and Aral seas on the north side of the Karakum desert in present-day Uzbekistan. The decision of a large number of people to relocate to a new land, an undertaking that in this instance involved traversing difficult desert terrain, seeking permission to settle, and interacting with the people already implanted on the land they wished to occupy, could not have been taken on a piecemeal basis. Nothing indicates a slow, family-by-family, Turkic infiltration of northeastern Iran. Debates must have been held; tribal leaders must have concurred on their course of action. Thus the climatic argument does not entirely deny the human factor. It simply raises the question of whether the key issues in the debates over migration turned on weather and livestock or on politics.

Two episodes of this migration, which was undoubtedly more drawn out in reality than it appears in the sources, are described briefly in histories of the period. The first episode took place during the first decade of the eleventh/last decade of the fourth century; that is, at the onset of the Big Chill. The second occurred twenty to twenty-five years later. In 1900 the Russian Orientalist Wilhelm Barthold, in his masterful *Turkestan Down to the Mongol Invasion,* subtly evaded the question of why the first migration occurred. After describing a conflict in Central Asia in which Oghuz warriors fought on the losing side against Sultan Mahmud of Ghazna, he says: "Mahmud first of all dealt with the Turkmen [i.e., Oghuz] allies of Ali-tagin, whose chief was Seljuk's son Isra'il. He succeeded in capturing Isra'il ... who was sent to India and there imprisoned in a fortress. His hordes were partly exterminated, but a number of them broke away from their leaders (the descendants of Seljuk), and *with Mahmud's consent emigrated to Khurasan"* (emphasis added).[1]

Most recently, a current scholar, drawing on the same fragments of narrative history that have remained unaugmented for the past century, reached essentially the same conclusion:

> But incidentally the Saljuqs did not exhibit any resentment on what Sultan Mahmud had done to Isra'il. Instead, acting under the command of Tughril and Chaghri [Isra'il's nephews], [they] made a submission to the sultan requesting him to allow them to cross the waters of Oxus and settle somewhere between Nasa and Abivard in order to have sufficient grazing grounds for their cattle [sic]. . . . Consequent upon this Sultan Mahmud acceded to their request and allotted them the grazing grounds in the steppe near Sarakhs, Abivard and Farava (Qizil Arvat). [2]

What is puzzling in this episode is that the military confrontation between Ali-tagin and Mahmud of Ghazna does not seem to have made the subsequent migration necessary. If anything, it suggests the contrary. That a defeated people might seek amnesty, or permission to return home, from a ruler who had decimated their forces and captured their leader is readily understandable. But why would they seek to resettle in the territory of the ruler who has just defeated them? And why would a ruler with any concern at all for military security look with favor on their petition to do so? There is no hint that Mahmud expected the Turkomans to join his army, as sometimes happens when a portion of a defeated force changes allegiance. Indeed, the historical record shows that far from becoming reliable supporters of the sultan after their resettlement, the Turkoman newcomers turned into marauders who greatly disturbed the peace of northern Iran (fig. 4.1).

One story asserts that this negative outcome was not unforeseen at the time: "Arsalan Jadhib the governor of Tus [the modern city of Mashhad near Nishapur], warned the Sultan against this [i.e., the resettlement of the Oghuz] and suggested either to eliminate all the Saljuqs or to get the thumbs of their male ones cut, so that they may [sic] not be able to operate the bows."[3]

The insufficiency of the political narrative in explaining the cause of the migration has encouraged broad generalizations in histories dealing with the

FIGURE 4.1.    Map of frontier between Iran and Central Asia.

transformative impact of Turkic tribes entering the Middle East. In his recent survey *The Turks in World History*, Carter Findley barely addresses the question:

> The Seljuks' origins lie clouded in the ethnogenesis of the Oghuz Turks [known in Arabic sources as Ghuzz], whose history of state formation began in the ninth century, prior to their conversion to Islam. The original Seljuk, a commander from the Kinik tribe of the Oghuz, converted to Islam in 985 at Jand on the Syr Darya (Jaxartes River). The biblical names of his four sons—Mika'il, Isra'il, Musa, and Yunus (Jonah)—suggest previous acquaintance with either Khazar Judaism or Nestorian Christianity.

Now, they and their followers [here Findley quotes the noted Central Asian historian Peter Golden] "became part of the Islamicized Turkic border population that warred with the 'pagans' in the steppe." *Pressured by tribal movements and political instability*, they were "universally described as a bedraggled, sorry lot, driven by desperation and impending starvation to conquest." Serving first one petty dynast and then another, under Mika'il's sons Toghrul and Chaghri, they migrated into Khurasan and began raiding the local populace. . . . Ghaznavid attempts to stop this led to battle at Dandanqan (23 May 1040[/9 Ramadan 431]), a victory of Seljuk desperation over Ghaznavid exhaustion. The Seljuks became masters of Khurasan, expanding their power into Transoxania and across Iran [emphasis added].[4]

Here "tribal movements and political instability" are presented as if they were factors that explained, rather than merely described, the Oghuz migration. The noted Iranian historian Anne Lambton follows a similar line: "The reasons leading to the migration of the Ghuzz into Khurasan and Kirman at the end of the Great Saljuq period were perhaps not very dissimilar to those which had brought about the migration of the Ghuzz into Persia rather over a century earlier: *shortage of pastures, political pressure, and perhaps over-population . . .*" (emphasis added).[5]

At the level of causation, the *southward* migration of the Oghuz thus becomes assimilated with a much-better-known succession of *westward* movements by earlier horse nomads of the steppe, such as the Huns, Avars, Magyars, Khazars, and Pechenegs. "Tribal movements and political instability" or "political pressure" affected them all. But the Oghuz alone migrated in a different direction: southward."

The Eurasian steppe is a belt of nearly continuous grassland running from the Danubian plain of Hungary, at its western end, to Mongolia and the doorway of China in the east. Ecologically, it is the counterpart of the Great Plains of North America and the Pampas of Argentina. Vast herds of wild horses once roamed the steppe, and it was there, more toward the west than the east, that populations of domestic horses first appeared.[6] The societies that exploited the resources of the steppe largely sustained themselves on the products of their livestock, not just horses, but also sheep, goats, and in suitable areas, cattle. In some regions, particularly toward the south, where mountains and deserts formed the steppe boundary, they also raised two-humped camels. These they used for carrying burdens, both camp goods, like collapsible huts, and trade goods along caravan routes, and occasionally for pulling carts. However, camels tended to be few in comparison to their other livestock, and they were only infrequently used for meat or milk. The nomads' pride was their horses, which gave them mobility and military potential. The grassy terrain was ideal for horses and offered few barriers to the movement of peoples eastward and westward.

But not southward. Seas and high mountains form the southern boundaries of the steppe, except in the region directly east of the Caspian Sea and currently within the borders of Turkmenistan and Uzbekistan. There deserts intervene between the lush grasslands and the arid but irrigable provinces of northern Iran and Afghanistan. The Karakum ("Black Sand") Desert extends from the east coast of the Caspian Sea to the west bank of the Oxus River (today the Amu Darya). Once across the Oxus, the desert resumes, with the Kizilkum ("Red Sand") Desert extending eastward from the river and angling a bit farther to the north. Four millennia ago, when the Indo-Iranian peoples are thought to have migrated south from Central Asia and are believed to have split, with some going east toward India and others west toward Mesopotamia, these deserts may not have been as dry and forbidding as they have since become. But even then it is unlikely that passage from Central Asia into Iran could have been made without traversing daunting desert terrain.

If aridity east of the Caspian subsequently increased, as some, but not all, climate historians maintain, southward migrations from the northern grasslands could only have become more difficult. Those known pastoral peoples who did make their way south, such as the Sakae (Scythians) in the second century BCE and the Hephthalites, or White Huns, in the fourth century CE, stayed close to sources of fresh water in the rivers that drained the snow-clad mountains of Afghanistan and Tajikistan before crossing the desert to be absorbed in the sands or empty into salt lakes. The Zeravshan River supplied water for the caravan cities of Samarqand and Bukhara and their surrounding farmlands. Its waters, however, sank into the earth and evaporated before reaching the Oxus River to the west. A much larger stream

than the Zeravshan, the Oxus made extensive canal irrigation possible in
Bactria (northern Afghanistan) before changing its direction of flow from
westward to northward, separating the Karakum and Kizilkum deserts,
and finally ending up in a fertile delta, where it debouched into the hyper-
saline Aral Sea. This fertile delta region in the midst of the desert became
known as Khwarazm. Continuing west, the next channel draining Afghanistan's mountains was the Murghab River, which formed a smaller arable
delta before disappearing into the sands just north of the city of Marv; and
then came the Tejen River, also known as the Hari Rud, which turned
north and passed by the city of Sarakhs before dwindling to nothing in the
wastes of Turkmenistan.

West of the Tejen River, which today forms a portion of the border between Iran and Turkmenistan, the mountains are much lower and drier than
those in Afghanistan and Tajikistan. Their snowmelt and occasional springs
produce a number of seasonal gully-washing streams that flow for a few miles
northward into the Karakum Desert, but in recent centuries qanat irrigation
has been used to exploit the limited agricultural potential of the piedmont.
(Soviet construction of an east–west canal from the Oxus River has brought
irrigation water to the desert and transformed southern Turkmenistan into a
cotton-producing agricultural region.)

The mountains not only are low, but are arrayed in a double range. The
Alborz, which has towering heights along the southern Caspian coast but
becomes comparatively low in its eastward extension, known as the Binalud,
is today entirely within Iran. The Kopet Dagh follows a parallel course just to
the north of the Binalud and today forms most of the border between Iran
and Turkmenistan. Runoff from the northern slopes of the Binalud and the
southern slopes of the Kopet Dagh does form a significant Iranian river, the
Atrak; but this flows westward into the Caspian Sea and thus affords no
route across the Karakum Desert.[7] As for the northern side of the Kopet
Dagh, Wilhelm Barthold, following the British traveler Lord Curzon, remarks: "Nothing can match the gloomy spectacle of these sterile heights of
gray limestone, watered only by a few springs and deprived of any vegetation
except sparse juniper."[8]

These geographical details come into historical focus when one takes into
account the specific places where the narratives of the period say the Oghuz

migrants either asked to be relocated or were granted grazing lands by Sultan Mahmud: Sarakhs, Abivard, Nasa, and Farava (modern Qizil Arvat in Turkmenistan). Beginning with Sarakhs at the Tejen River border between Iran and Turkmenistan, these four towns (Farava actually less a town than a fortified defense community surrounded by sands) form a straight line along the narrow band of foothills that separates the northern slopes of the Kopet Dagh from the Karakum Desert. In the words of a modern geographer: "Between the mountains and the desert lowlands is the piedmont, which is characterized by a hilly zone up to twelve miles wide and a gently rolling alluvial plain, varying in width from a few miles to twenty miles."[9]

The most eloquent Iranian historian of the early eleventh/fifth century, Abu al-Fazl Bayhaqi, worked as a secretary for Mahmud of Ghazna's son and successor, Sultan Mas'ud. He was thus a firsthand observer of many of the events he wrote about. We shall encounter his description of the second episode of Oghuz migration later. What is relevant here is an observation he puts into the mouth of his master in 1035/426, when Sultan Mas'ud is deciding to resist a request by the Seljuq chieftains Tughril and Chaghri to bring thousands more Oghuz Turkomans into Khurasan: "[O]ne must remember what mischief and trouble were brought by . . . those Turkmens whom my father [Sultan Mahmud] allowed in and brought over the [Oxus] river and gave a place within Khorasan, where they lived as camel herders (*sarbanan*)."[10]

This one word, *sarbanan*, "camel herders," shines a light on the Oghuz migration that historians focused on the political narrative have chosen to ignore. Although there is no denying that the Turkomans had herds of horses that they rode into battle, they did not act like paradigmatic steppe horse-herders in specifying where they wanted to live. The horse nomads who moved southward from Central Asia in earlier times had followed the rivers across the desert and eventually found new homes in good horse country on the upper reaches of the rivers, mostly in northern Afghanistan (the districts of Balkh [Bactria], Juzjan, Gharchistan, and Badghis). Or they had headed still farther south into the arid but spacious plains of Sijistan (from Sakastanae = "land of the Sakae") in eastern Iran, or even farther toward the valley of the Indus River in Pakistan. For several thousand years, no one had specifically sought land on the desert fringe of the Kopet Dagh piedmont, an area that Muslim cartographers would come to label *mafaza Ghuzz*, the "Ghuzz (Oghuz) Frontier." To be sure, horse nomads could find adequate pasture just a bit further to the south in the valley of the Atrak River between the Binalud Mountains and the Kopet Dagh, but the narrow strip of land between the northern slopes and the desert could not be considered prime horse country.[11] Barthold, following the first-century CE writer Strabo, remarks: "In Achaemenid times, the region did not have much importance; according to Strabo, the Persian kings, during their tours of the country, strove to pass through Parthia [the name then of the Turkmenistan frontier] as quickly as possible, because the region was too poor to sustain their large retinues."[12] In short, the Oghuz who beseeched Sultan Mahmud for a new place to live were seeking to move into camel country, not horse country.

What the Oghuz relocation amounted to was a move from the northern fringe of the Karakum Desert between the Aral Sea and the Caspian Sea to the southern fringe of the same desert. The north–south distance across the desert is only some 150 miles at its western end along the Caspian coast. But the Caspian is a saltwater lake; there was too little fresh water on this route for a full-scale folk migration with large herds of animals.

Historically, raiding parties had used this western route when they wanted to attack the towns and villages on the warm and fertile Gorgan plain at the southeast corner of the sea. The Balkhan Mountains near the barren seashore had water and thus afforded them an intermediate stopping point. The antiquity of this route being used for cross-desert raiding is testified to by a wall built to defend the lowlands, the so-called Wall of Alexander, which dates in its earliest form to the Parthian period (third century BCE–third century CE).

Farther to the east, the distance between Khwarazm, the canal-irrigated delta of the Oxus River, and the Kopet Dagh range is more than 300 miles. A track across the wastes from Farawa to Khwarazm existed, but the country it traversed was exceedingly dry and barren desert. It too would have lacked the fresh water needed for a full-scale folk migration.

The route followed by the Oghuz, therefore, lay still farther to the east, as indicated by Bayhaqi's reference to crossing the Oxus River. Assuming the thousands of migrants with their flocks and herds were coming from the Khwarazm area, they would have followed the Oxus River upstream; that is, southeastward, for about 300 miles until it intersected the segment of the Silk Road linking the river with the town of Sarakhs on the Tejen River to the southwest. The distance from the Oxus to Sarakhs was about 150 miles, but there was ample fresh water at either end, and as a major caravan route, the way was well provided with stopping and watering points. The Sarakhs area, where some Oghuz reportedly received grazing lands, was not only an important stop on a busy caravan route, but also a well-known center for camel breeding. An anonymous Persian geography of 982/372 describes Sarakhs as follows: "A town lying on the road amid a steppe. [The word translated as 'steppe,' *biyaban*, normally means 'desert.'] A dry river-bed passes through the market; the water flows in it only at the time of floods. It is a place with much cultivation, and its people are strongly built and warlike. Camels are their wealth."[13]

Most of the Turkomans who arrived at Sarakhs passed on to the west, to Abivard, Nasa, and Farava. That this was specifically planned can be deduced from the fact that three decades or so later, during the second Oghuz migration in 1035/426, the Seljuq chieftains Tughril, Chaghri, and Yabghu were formally granted authority over three places: Dihistan, Farava, and Nasa. Dihistan on the Atrak River near the Caspian Sea was even farther to the west than Farava, indicating that the Turkoman migration resulted in their becoming a pastoral presence all the way from Sarakhs to the sea. The anonymous geographer of 982/372, writing more than two decades before the first Oghuz migration, when raiders from the northern side of the Karakum Desert were the paramount concern, described Dihistan as "a frontier post (*thaghr*) against (*bar ruy*) the Ghuz [sic]."[14] He used the same phrase as part of his description of Farava: "A *ribat* [fortress], situated on the frontier between Khorasan and Dihistan, on the edge of the desert. It is a frontier post against the Ghuz [sic]. Within the *ribat* there is a spring of water sufficient for drinking purposes. The inhabitants have no fields, and bring grain from Nasa and Dihistan."[15]

Camel herding affords an entirely plausible rationale for the Oghuz itinerary. The terrain matched the sort of desert grazing their animals had long been accustomed to on the north side of the desert, and they were undoubtedly familiar with the lands they were heading toward from having raided them in earlier times. With respect to the first migratory episode,

however, geography does not explain why the Turkomans chose not to return
to their customary lands after their battlefield defeat at the hands of Sultan
Mahmud. There may have been unmentioned political problems about returning home. In the absence of any specific information, however, we will
pursue the hypothesis that they moved from the north side to the south side
of the Karakum Desert because increasingly frigid winters were endangering
their camels. According to modern data, the mean January temperature of
the old Oghuz grazing lands west of the Aral Sea is 12 to 15 degrees Celsius
colder than the temperatures in the desert lowlands southeast of the Caspian
Sea. For camel breeders facing a deteriorating climate, this difference would
have been crucial.

Over the past four decades I have thought about and written about scores of
historical questions relating to domesticated camels.[16] To the best of my
knowledge, however, the history of the geographical dividing line between
one-humped camels and two-humped camels has never been thoroughly explored. On the one hand, scholars more or less agree that the species found in
(northern) Iran and Central Asia in ancient times had two humps. At some
point, however, the territory of the one-humped camel expanded to encompass all of Iran, Afghanistan south of the Hindu Kush Mountains, and most
of Pakistan and northern India. Inasmuch as the animals were all domestic,
this expansion must have been the product of human decisions and the activities of human groups. Were the decisions based on transport and commerce or on patterns of nomadic subsistence? The records are silent. Were the
groups involved Arab? Iranian? Baluch? Afghan? Turkic? Again, no specific
answer from the narrative sources.

The part of this extensive but unknown history that we are concerned
with here pertains to the fact that for hundreds of years, and still today, the
camel population of the southern Karakum Desert in Turkmenistan has
been of the one-humped variety. Farther north and farther east, two-humped
camels become the norm. Indeed, Turkmenistan represents the northern extreme of one-humped camel breeding. In considering the possible effects of
climatic deterioration on the livelihood of pastoral nomads, therefore, we

must recognize that, unlike the cold-adapted livestock commonly kept by the nomads of the Eurasian steppe—horses, cattle, sheep, goats, two-humped camels—the domestic one-humped camel was native to the torrid deserts of Arabia.

I know of no extensive scientific study of the effects of cold on one-humped camels. However, an essay on the Arvana breed of Turkmenistan available on an encyclopedic website devoted to animal breeds, and repeated verbatim on a Turkmenistan public relations website, maintains, citing a scientific source, that "Arvana camels are not adapted to severe winters."[17] Even so, I would not consider the findings of a modern field study conclusive with respect to the camel populations of the early Islamic centuries, because many breeds and subbreeds have developed in different environmental regions over the past 1400 years. For the period we are dealing with, the best testimony comes from the preeminent medieval authority on animals, ʿAmr b. Bahr al-Jahiz, an Iraqi of Abyssinian descent who died in 868/255. At one point in his voluminous *Kitab al-Hayawan*, or "Book of Animals," he remarks: "Camels die in the land of Rum [Anatolia or central Turkey]. They perish and their condition becomes bad."[18] Again he says: "It is wonderful how the men of Rum enjoy peaceful relations with the camel nomads knowing that the entry of camels into the land of Rum leads to their death."[19] To this testimony can be added the previously cited story heard by the traveler Ibn Fadlan in 921/308, when frigid weather stranded him and his embassy in Khwarazm for three months: "Two men took twelve camels out to collect wood in some brushy swamps. . . . When they awoke after spending the night in the cold, they found that all of the camels had frozen to death."[20] Though this story may have been exaggerated, it is noteworthy that it involves one-humped camels—using *jamal*, the standard Arabic word—rather than horses, mules, or two-humped beasts. It seems highly unlikely that such a story would have come to Ibn Fadlan's ears if the local people who told it to him had not deemed it at least minimally credible.

The southern edge of the Karakum Desert to which the Oghuz relocated is at the same latitude as the frontier between northern Mesopotamia and Anatolia that al-Jahiz identifies as the northern limit for the herds of the Arab camel nomads, the cousins of the Arabs who formed the first Muslim presence in Khurasan and Central Asia. The Land of Rum, where camels perish,

is somewhat farther north, but not as far as the northern edge of the Karakum Desert, which is on the same latitude as the southern Black Sea. Although the central plains of Anatolia are higher in altitude than the Karakum Desert and have probably always been colder in winter, it is evident that
if the camels of Turkmenistan were at that time of the one-humped variety
known to al-Jahiz, then they were living at the extreme northern limit of
their physiological range. (In later centuries, more cold-adapted one-humped
camels with thick, woolly coats, referred to as Turkoman camels and seemingly identical to the modern Arvana of Turkmenistan, did become known
in the Land of Rum; but as we shall see, they were probably introduced there
by the Oghuz.)

Large numbers of one-humped camels came to Turkmenistan with the
Arab armies at the time of the Islamic conquests. According to early chronicles, tens of thousands of Arabs migrated to Khurasan, and the largest number settled in the army encampment of Marv. Located on the delta of the
Murghab River, where canal irrigation made farming possible, Marv was
otherwise surrounded by desert. It therefore had an abundance of desert
grazing for the Arabs' camels, which may well have played a role in its being
selected as the principal Muslim military strongpoint on the Central Asian
frontier. A second Arab military camp at Balkh in northern Afghanistan
similarly received a large number of camels.

Yet one-humped camels, presumably from Mesopotamia, were not entirely
unknown in the trade entrepots of the Silk Road at the time of the Arabs' arrival. A wall painting from Samarqand depicts what is probably a funeral procession for a mid-seventh-century Sogdian king.[21] A diminutive white elephant
with a female rider leads the procession followed by three ladies on horseback. After them come two bearded men mounted on one-humped camels and
carrying what appear to be ornate ceremonial batons (fig. 4.2). Additional evidence comes from excavations at Ak Tepe near Marv that have yielded a clay
seal impression of the late Sasanid period showing a one-humped camel.[22]
Nevertheless, the one-humped animals were undoubtedly uncommon. Not
only does the appearance of two camels and a white elephant as ceremonial
steeds in a ritual procession hint that all three animals were exotic (the sixteen other mounts in the Samarqand procession are all horses), but contemporary silver coins minted in Khwarazm on the Aral Sea adjoining the north-

FIGURE 4.2.    Camel riders from pre-Islamic fresco in Samarqand. (By permission of Markus
Mode, Department of Oriental Architecture and Art, Halle-Wittenberg.)

ern Karakum Desert show two-humped camels, which makes it quite certain
that this was the dominant camel species then found in Turkmenistan.[23]

Were the people who bred the two-humped camels of pre-Islamic Khwarazm Turkomans or Khwarazmians? The latter, who are known to have
spoken an Iranian language, are usually assumed to be the sedentary farming
people of the Oxus River delta. Most of the pastoralists encountered by the
invading Arabs are described as Turks. In either case, it is certain that two-
humped camel herding was well established before the Arabs conquered the
region and established Marv, farther to the south on the Murghab River
delta, as their primary military cantonment. Needless to say, many of the
Arabs who settled there, and a bit later in Balkh, came from camel-breeding
tribes in Arabia.

Because in modern times all the camels of Turkmenistan, and of the scat-
tered Turkoman-peopled areas on the Iranian side of the border, have but one
hump, the question arises of when and why the changeover from the prevailing
two-humped species took place. The most suggestive textual source is a statement in the *Kitab al-Buldan*, "Book of Lands," by Ahmad al-Ya'qubi, who died

in 897/283, long before the climate began to cool. Speaking of the Gorgan area at the southeastern corner of the Caspian Sea (i.e., in almost the same area as that to which the Oghuz began to migrate in the early eleventh/fifth century), he says it has *al-ibil al-bukhati al-ʿizami*, or "huge *bukhati* camels."[24]

The Arabic adjective *bukhati* comes from a plural of the word *bukht*. Al-Jahiz is inconsistent in his use of *bukht*. Sometimes it means a two-humped camel, but normally it denotes the hybrid animal produced by crossing a one-humped camel with a two-humped camel.[25] The *bukht* was notably larger and stronger than either parent, as Yaʿqubi indicates by the word *ʿizam* ("great, huge"), and it was therefore an ideal baggage camel for the western segment of the Silk Road, where it passed from frigid Central Asia into the warmer lands of Iran and Iraq. The female hybrid, called a *jammaza*, was particularly good for riding and is sometimes defined as "a swift riding camel." (Both animals looked superficially to be one-humped in that they had one large mound on their backs (fig. 4.3), but some mounds had a 2- to 6-inch indentation approximately a third of the way back from the shoulders, representing the missing gap between the humps.) Al-Jahiz summarized the breeding as follows:

> When [male] two-humped camels (*al-fawalij*) are bred with [female] Arab camels (*[al-ibil] al-ʿirab*), you get these noble [*karima*] *bukhts* and *jammazas* that combine the virtues of the Arab with the virtues of the *bukht* [here meaning "two-humped camel"]. For the conformation of these two species does not get any nobler, more glorious, more pleasing, or more costly. But when you mate the Arab stallions with the females of the *bukht* [apparently meaning the first-generation hybrid], you get the *bahwaniya* and [*sarsaraniya*] camels. In appearance they are uglier than their two parents and in tightness of conformation [*asran*] more crabbed [*ashadda*].[26]

According to a number of sources, when a hybrid was bred with either a one-humped or two-humped mate, the configuration of the offspring, at least with respect to the number of humps, reverted to that of the non-hybrid parent. And when hybrids were mated with each other, the offspring were not viable.[27] For this reason adult hybrids were never part of breeding herds.

FIGURE 4.3.    Hybrid camel breeding herd. The second animal from the left has the
indented mound on the back and long hair characteristic of a bukht.
(Photo by Michael Bonine.)

When the *bukhts* and *jammazas* became old enough, they were sold off as baggage or riding animals. This not only brought a significant profit to those pastoralists that specialized in breeding hybrids, but it made them prime livestock suppliers for the caravan trade and the military.

Geographically, the Oghuz of the Khwarazm region were perfectly situated to become breeders of hybrid camels for Silk Road caravans. The large herds of one-humped females that they needed could not have been hard to come by once the Arabs stationed a large army in Marv and a smaller one near the Caspian Sea in Gorgan. The two-humped sires the Turkomans already had. And the fringes of the Karakum Desert offered excellent grazing lands that no other people would ever covet, since they were too meager to support enormous horse herds. Furthermore, the Turkomans had easy access to the major Silk Road entrepot of Bukhara. Along with Samarqand, which was closer to Balkh (see later), Bukhara seems to have been a transshipment point where caravans of two-humped camels from China unloaded their goods. These were then reloaded onto hybrid *bukhts* for the onward journey through Iran and Iraq.

There is no way of proving from current textual evidence that some of the Oghuz did, in fact, specialize in breeding hybrids as a commercial product. But those that lived in the vicinity of Khwarazm were certainly camel breeders. Ibn Fadlan makes this evident when he remarks that his embassy bought "Turkish camels" when they passed from Khwarazm into the territory of the Oghuz.[28] Though the Arabic word that he uses, *jamal*, properly refers to one-humped animals, the adjective *Turkish* implies a different breed than the one Ibn Fadlan was familiar with from his home in Iraq. Was this his way of referring to a hybrid? Possibly so, since his Arab readers back home would almost certainly have been unfamiliar with the word *bukht*. Or were these "Turkish camels" that carried their riders through knee-deep snow simply a local breed like the modern Turkoman camel that had been bred to resist cold conditions better than the conventional one-humped beast?

The geographers' descriptions of the locales chosen for resettlement by the groups of Oghuz that moved south raise the possibility of hybrid breeding more explicitly. The previously cited references to the Silk Road town of Sarakhs as a locale surrounded by the Karakum sands whose wealth was in camels, and to Gorgan as a place where hybrids were bred both antedate the southward migration of the Oghuz, which suggests that the Arabs, who had originally brought one-humped camels to northeastern Iran, were probably the first to profit from this breeding industry. Moreover, the one other eastern area where *bukhts* and *jammazas* were explicitly bred seems to have been a gold mine for local Arab nomads. Pastoralists around Balkh, the Arab garrison city far to the east in northern Afghanistan, also produced hybrids.[29] Like Gorgan and Marv (though not Sarakhs), Balkh had become a major Arab military center in the eighth/second century, and the Arabs had brought their one-humped camels with them. All they had to do was interbreed the females with the locally available two-humped males. According to the anonymous tenth-/fourth-century Persian geographer, the deserts just to the west of Balkh were home to some 20,000 Arabs who raised camels and sheep. He pointedly adds that these were the richest Arabs in all of Khurasan.[30] The source of their riches is self-evident.

The strongest likelihood, therefore, is that the Oghuz groups living in the northern Karakum Desert adopted the breeding of hybrids in the ninth/third century from the Arabs on the south side of the desert whose territory they regularly raided. Their original stock may well have been stolen from the Arabs and driven northward across the desert when the raiding party returned home. And one might further conjecture that when the sons of Seljuq and their tribal followers became fully engaged in the commercial production of hybrid camels, and apparently became at least nominal Muslims, their most obvious market would have been to provide pack animals for the Silk Road caravaneers in nearby Bukhara.

Such a scenario could explain two puzzles in the sources. First, the abundance of Biblical names among the descendants of Seljuq suggests, as Carter Findley noted, a possible connection with either the Jewish Khazar Turks at the mouth of the Volga River on the northern coast of the Caspian Sea or the Nestorian Christian Uighur Turks, who were very active as Silk Road traders. If the Oghuz did breed hybrids, the considerations outlined earlier would clearly point to the Silk Road and Nestorian Christianity as the more likely source of scriptural names and thereby suggest that the Seljuq family was more than casually involved in the culture and commerce of that great trade route. We will return to this possibility in the next chapter.

Second, the seemingly unwise decision of Sultan Mahmud to grant the Oghuz permission to move to the southern edge of the Karakum Desert would become eminently plausible. By acceding to their request for grazing lands he probably thought that he was gaining access to a major source of high-quality animals, not just for caravan use, but also for his army. Bayhaqi's history has many references to the thousands of hybrid *jammazas* used for Ghaznavid military campaigns, including a string of incursions into then camel-free northern India that would have required thousands of baggage animals. The Arab nomads living west of Balkh undoubtedly supplied many of the needed baggagers and remounts. But during the years when Mahmud and his son Mas'ud were disputing territory with Turkic chieftains on the Khurasan frontier in Central Asia, having a reliable western source for army remounts and baggagers would have been highly desirable.

For further clues we must look at the circumstances surrounding the second Oghuz migration to the southern edge of the Karakum in 1034/426. In that year, after losing one of his commanders in a battle with the Turkomans, the Ghaznavid ruler, Sultan Mas'ud, gave an angry order: "The Commander-in-Chief must go with an army and hem in these brutish camel-drivers and give them a drubbing and then proceed to Balkh."[31] The term *camel-drivers* (*sarbanan*) clearly has a pejorative meaning in this passage, but this does not mean that it was inaccurate. Later that same year Bayhaqi quotes Sultan Mas'ud as follows:

> Ten thousand Turkish horsemen, with many leaders, have come, planted themselves in the midst of our province with their avowed grievance that there is no place of refuge for them while in truth it is we who have become afflicted. For our part, we shall not allow them to settle on the land and grow in size and strength, for one must remember what mischief and trouble were brought by . . . those Turkmens whom my father allowed in and brought over the river and gave a place within Khorasan, where they lived as camel herders (*sarbanan*). We cannot allow these people, whom the Vizier says are lusting after territory, to remain there and to take their ease there.[32]

In this passage, part of which was cited earlier, the Turkomans facing Mas'ud are explicitly likened to the Oghuz bands that were admitted into Khurasan in the time of Mas'ud's father, Sultan Mahmud of Ghazna. The term *camel herders* is used here as a simple description rather than as an insult. "Camel herders" may have been lowly in the eyes of the sultan, but Mas'ud's pugnacious invective in no way dissociates his enemies from camel breeding. In fact, it gives a context for the Oghuz claim that they had "no place of refuge." Bayhaqi expands on that claim by giving the text of a letter sent by the Seljuq leaders to Abu al-Fazl Suri, one of Mas'ud's military commanders:

> To the lofty presence of the exalted Sheykh, the Master, the Sayyid, our lord Abu'l-Fazl Suri b. al-Mo'tazz, from the slaves Yabghu, Toghril and Davud [the Seljuq chiefs], clients (*mavali*) of the Commander of the Faithful [the caliph in Baghdad].
>
> It was not possible for us slaves to remain at Bukhara in Transoxania. While 'Alitegin was alive, we enjoyed a mutually harmonious and friendly relationship, but now that he is dead, we have to deal with his sons, both very young and green. . . . Khwarazm fell into a very disturbed

state with the killing of Harun, and it was not possible for us to move there. We have come for protection to the Lord of the World, the Great Sultan, the Dispenser of Favors, so that the Khwaja, Suri, might act as a mediator and might write to the Grand Vizier . . . and intercede with him, since there is a bond of friendship between him and us. *Every winter, the Khwarazm Shah Altuntash, may God have mercy on him, used to allot us, our families and our beasts a place within his province until springtime, and the Grand Vizier used to act as intercessor.* If the exalted judgment sees fit, we can be admitted as submissive vassals in such a way that one of us could be serving at the exalted court, while the others could undertake whatever task the lord may command; and we shall be able to shelter under his mighty shadow. *The district of Nasa and Farava, which borders the desert, could be bestowed on us so that we may deposit our baggage and impedimenta there and feel free from cares and worries. We will not allow any evildoer from Balkhan Kuh* [the mountains north of Dihistan near the Caspian coast], *Dehestan, the fringes of Khwarazm or the regions adjacent to the Oxus to cause trouble, and we will drive away the Iraqi and Khwarazmian Turkmens.* If, God forbid, the lord does not give us a favorable answer, we do not know what will happen for we have no place on earth and there is nowhere left for us. We did not dare to write anything directly to that august court, given its overpowering splendor, so we wrote to the Khwaja in order that he might bring this matter to a conclusion in a masterful fashion, if God, He is exalted and magnified, so wills [emphasis added].[33]

Given the pleading nature of this entreaty by the Seljuq chiefs, the details in this letter may not be entirely accurate. But Bayhaqi, who was a firsthand observer throughout this period, obviously believed their story. In an undated portion of his chronicle devoted to the district of Khwarazm, he repeats the same information in summary form:

Following the events in Khwarazm and Harun's plight, the Seljuqs became even more despondent about their own future: they could not go to Bokhara, since 'Alitegin had died, and his sons, a hopeless lot, had assumed power there; nor could they stay in Khwarazm out of fear of Shah

Malek. So they thought of moving from Khwarazm into Khorasan and seeking refuge there. Their people were all ready and prepared, so they suddenly moved off and crossed the Oxus. On that day, there were 700 horsemen who crossed the river, and then afterwards, large numbers joined up with them. They ... came to the region of Merv and Nasa, and installed themselves there.[34]

Both of these documents state that the Oghuz considered the districts of Khwarazm and Bukhara to be their normal territories, with the former specifically being their winter pasture. The contemporary geographers, however, do not mention Bukhara in connection with the Oghuz. Ibn Hawqal places them this way: "to the west [of Khurasan] is found the Desert of the Ghuzz and the districts of Gorgan."[35] This placement is affirmed in a cartographic tradition that gives the label *bilad Ghuzziya,* or "country of the Ghuzz," to the northern portion of the Karakum Desert, the area indicated by Ibn Hawqal.[36] The specification of a summer migration to Bukhara, therefore, probably reflects an elevated demand for caravan animals specific to that postcalving season. Khwarazm, unlike Bukhara, was well removed from the main Silk Road traffic, and so presumably from the related animal marketing.

Be that as it may, the question of "seeking refuge," as Bayhaqi presents it, is explicitly narrated as a consequence of political friction, not of cold winters. The current rulers in Bukhara and Khwarazm are represented as so unfriendly that the Seljuqs had no choice but to find somewhere else to go. Yet they did not want to go wherever the sultan might suggest. They wanted to go to precisely the same districts that the Oghuz had migrated to—and disrupted—more than two decades earlier. Moreover, they recognized that those earlier Oghuz had turned into plunderers, and they offered to defend Mas'ud's realm from their depredations.

Mas'ud rejected this petition and chose to fight. This decision led ultimately to the Battle of Dandanqan in 1040/431, where the Turkomans thoroughly thrashed his army. After that, Mas'ud and his Ghaznavid successors focused their attention on the Indian portion of their empire and left Khurasan to be ruled by the Seljuqs. In this way, two episodes of Turkomans seeking refuge—not invading—along the southern fringes of the Karakum Desert became a turning point in world history.

Whether or not cold winters threatened the livelihood of camel breeders with vulnerable and valuable herds of one-humped and hybrid animals, and whether or not this threat weighed as heavily as politics in the decision of the Oghuz chieftains to lead their people south must remain a matter of conjecture. Yet it would be premature to end our discussion of climatic change on this indefinite note. If one gives even partial credence to the maximal interpretation of the Mongolian tree-ring data, which indicate some 130 years of comparatively cold winters starting in the first decade of the eleventh/last decade of the fourth century, the impact of climate on Seljuq economic and cultural history needs to be explored more broadly.

Though disparaging characterizations like those of Bayhaqi portray the early Seljuqs, in Peter Golden's words, as "a bedraggled, sorry lot, driven by desperation and impending starvation to conquest," and their rise to power in Khurasan as, in Carter Findley's words, "a victory of Seljuk desperation over Ghaznavid exhaustion," history remembers the Seljuqs as restorers of a degree of Muslim imperial unity not seen for more than 200 years. Though a comprehensive account of the Great Seljuq Empire has not yet been written, modern historians commonly recognize the Seljuq period as one of exceptional dynamism in politics, art, culture, and religious affairs.[37]

Yet they have little of a positive nature to say about the period after the death of the Sultan Sanjar in 1157/551, when family infighting, opportunistic local warlords, and rampaging tribes ended Seljuq unity once and for all. A successor regime based on Khwarazm and ruled by a Turkic family originally appointed by the Seljuqs eventually gained control over much of Iran. Like the Seljuqs, the Khwarazmshahs' power rested on tribal cavalry, as did the Turko-Mongol army of Genghiz Khan that destroyed the Khwarazmian "empire" when it invaded Iran in 615/1219. However, the land that they ruled, and that the Mongols subsequently ravaged, was already in a state of severe economic decline.

One way of assessing the difference between the Seljuq and Khwarazmian periods is to survey the world of Muslim religious scholarship and measure the changing proportion of scholars and dignitaries coming from Iran. Two famous Syrian compilers of scholarly biographies, Ibn al-ʿImad (d. 1687/1098) and al-Dhahabi (d. 1348/748), organized their works by death date and extended their coverage to the entire Muslim world.[38] They lived in different centuries and adhered to competing legal schools, the former being Hanbali and the latter Shafiʿi, and they included substantially different numbers of Iranian names in their works. Nevertheless, the proportions of biographies ascribable to Iranians in each twenty-five-year time period are almost identical, within one or two percentage points. This enhances the likelihood that their works actually reflect changes over time in the regional distribution of Muslim religious scholars and are not based on personal editorial preferences or the happenstance of what earlier compilations were available for their consultation. Table 4.1 is based on the compilation of Ibn al-ʿImad. Sixty years have been subtracted from the death dates he records to approximate dates of birth, because the social and economic climate of the society that nurtures noteworthy achievement in a young man is of greater relevance to us than the state of that society at the time of his death. The second column gives the total number of geographically locatable biographies in each twenty-five-year period.

The beginning of Iran's boom period coincides with a major jump in the proportion of Iranians entering into the cosmopolitan world of religious scholarship. Between the beginning of the ninth/third century and the end of the eleventh/fifth century, Iran's contribution of notable scholars to the Muslim faith community in general ranges between one third and one half. In the tenth/fourth and eleventh/fifth centuries Iran regularly edges out the capital province of Iraq as the most important region of Muslim learning.

The Big Chill initially causes no decline. Just as the greatest works of the Italian Renaissance date from after the phenomenal rise of the commercial city-states in the twelfth/sixth century, and after the demographic catastrophe of the Black Death in the middle of the following century, Iran's culture remained vigorous and creative despite the arrival of hard times. But it could not sustain its vitality through the period of Seljuq decline and Khwarazmian rule. Iranians born between 1170/566 and 1193/590, who were already well embarked on their careers before the Mongol invasion, account for less than half the proportion of Muslim scholars of a half century earlier.

TABLE 4.1    Proportion of Muslim scholars coming from Iran and Iraq

| BIRTHDATES | TOTAL | IRAN | IRAQ | COMMENTS |
|---|---|---|---|---|
| 709/91 | 161 | 9% | 46% | |
| 734/116 | 180 | 8% | 61% | <Abbasids come to power |
| 758/141 | 199 | 12% | 62% | |
| 782/166 | 213 | 24% | 54% | |
| 806/191 | 133 | 38% | 39% | < Cotton boom begins |
| 831/216 | 136 | 32% | 48% | |
| 855/241 | 186 | 38% | 39% | |
| 879/266 | 185 | 37% | 39% | |
| 903/291 | 184 | 40% | 36% | |
| 928/316 | 173 | 36% | 42% | <First cold snap |
| 952/341 | 168 | 41% | 32% | |
| 976/366 | 144 | 39% | 31% | |
| 1000/391 | 123 | 51% | 22% | <Big Chill begins |
| 1025/416 | 154 | 49% | 29% | <Seljuqs come to power |
| 1049/441 | 127 | 39% | 34% | |
| 1073/466 | 159 | 36% | 33% | |
| 1097/491 | 151 | 32% | 32% | <Seljuq family disorders |
| 1122/516 | 189 | 23% | 37% | |
| 1146/541 | 193 | 23% | 39% | |
| 1170/566 | 228 | 14% | 29% | <Post-Sanjar period |
| 1194/591 | 192 | 6% | 17% | |
| 1219/616 | 219 | 8% | 12% | <Mongol invasion |

These figures, it should be noted, are not as definitive as they appear to be. The provincial identifications on which they are based come largely from geographical epithets (*nisbas*) incorporated in the personal names of scholars (e.g., names like Baghdadi, Shirazi, and Isfahani). By the late Seljuq period, many of the Iranians who show up in the biographical dictionaries had already left Iran and were living in other provinces. Yet they were still known by their Iranian *nisbas*. So the huge drop in Iranian biographies for the Khwarazmian period actually reflects a deterioration in Iranian cultural affairs that set in while the Seljuqs were still in power. In other words, a more precise general appraisal of the Seljuq period would be that Iran was flourishing as a religious center when the Seljuqs came to power, and continued to flourish well into their rule, but it had fallen into a deep cultural slump by the time their empire finally fell apart.

We have proposed, of course, that a century-long Big Chill badly damaged the agricultural economy of northern Iran. The question here is how this damage might have affected other dimensions of Iranian life. For example, scores of incidents of severe factional turmoil wracked the cities of northern Iran during the period, and members of the religious scholarly elite played an active role in these confrontations. In earlier writings I have speculated about the causes of this ferocious factionalism.[39] Since becoming aware of the evidence for a long-term change in the climate, however, I would now suggest that whatever the ideological roots or religious orientations of the factions involved in the turmoil, a competition for resources under deteriorating economic circumstances, particularly experienced in big cities, may help explain the growing virulence of their rivalry in the late Seljuq period. Though factional hostility was already in evidence in the tenth/fourth century before the Big Chill began, its expression was generally limited to riots and personal assaults. But by 1160/555 large parts of some cities, most notably Nishapur, had been so ravaged and destroyed that they were all but abandoned. Factional warfare was not the sole cause of the destruction, but the other major cause, depredations by uncontrolled bands of Turkoman nomads, can also be plausibly related to deteriorating living conditions in the countryside.

Family histories patched together from individual entries in biographical dictionaries indicate that many individuals who had the means to leave Iran, and the skills in the Arabic language and the Islamic religious sciences needed to pursue high-level careers elsewhere, emigrated during this period.[40] At the same time, pastoral nomadism, a form of land exploitation based on sparse population, supplanted agriculture as the dominant rural activity in some areas. Yet quantifiable sources for testing the extent of Iranian depopulation in percentage terms are lacking.

One avenue of research that could help corroborate the idea that climate change had a strong negative impact on food production and demography is the history of non-Muslim lands where winters were also influenced by the Siberian High. The Big Chill should have affected Byzantine Anatolia, Armenia, and Kievan Russia as well as Iran and Central Asia. Concerning the former, "it is commonly held that after the middle of the eleventh century the empire suffered a continuous population decline."[41] This is also a period of substantial migration of Armenians from their traditional home in the highlands of eastern Anatolia to the warm lowlands of Cilicia, the modern Turkish province of Çukurova, where they established the Kingdom of Little Armenia in 1187/582. Russia too had a series of famines and revolts during the period.[42] Confirmation that the Big Chill played a role in any or all of these developments is beyond the scope of this book. However, if significant correlations should be found, the easy spread of Oghuz nomads throughout Anatolia before and after the Battle of Manzikert in 1071/463 might become more understandable.

Be that as it may, for the Seljuqs a paradox remains. At least in the early decades of their rule, they presided over a seemingly prosperous Iranian domain that faced no external military challenges. Yet climatic deterioration seems to have been steadily undermining the agricultural economy, and the new rulers had no experience with agriculture. One way to understand this seeming paradox might be to ascribe uncommonly skillful and effective leadership to the Iranian viziers the sultans engaged to administer their realm.[43] However, a look at a later episode of sudden change to nomadic rule, namely, the rise of the Mongol Ilkhan state in the thirteenth/seventh century, suggests a different interpretation. In both China and Iran, in the early stages of Mongol rule, taxes were mercilessly extorted from the peasantry with no comprehension of the negative long-term effects on agriculture. Yet at the same time the Mongol rulers strongly encouraged trade, particularly along the Silk Road. This was an activity they both understood and profited from directly, and the abundance of trade lent an aura of glittering prosperity to an empire whose agricultural sector was suffering badly.

Perhaps the Seljuqs acted in similar fashion. Al-Ghazali's letter to Sultan Sanjar pleading with him not to extort more from the citizens of Tus suggests as much. Being unfamiliar with agriculture, and certainly unaware of the problems unusually cold winters posed for farmers, the sultans may have simply taken what they could from the peasantry and done nothing to foster or restore productivity. What they did understand, however, if the discussion above of Oghuz camel-breeding is correct, was caravan trade. This contributed disproportionately to the early Seljuq prosperity, as it would later contribute to the luster of the Ilkhanid court.

The evidence for Seljuq concentration on long-distance trade takes several forms. The reappearance of ulama professional names relating to Central Asian trade commodities like felt, fur, and silk was mentioned in chapter 3. In art it has often been noticed that the faces painted by Seljuq period artists have a strong East Asian appearance that was not previously present. The costumes depicted also point to a renewal of Silk Road commerce. Silk brocade becomes the standard apparel for elite individuals. The garments do not replicate the patterns of the Sasanid era, but they reflect a renewal of the Sasanid taste for Silk Road luxuries and confirm the decline of cotton as a high-status fabric for civil dignitaries that had already begun in the tenth/ fourth century.

A further indication that high-value trade played an enhanced role in Seljuq times can be found in the plentiful minting of Seljuq gold dinars and the relative scarcity of silver dirhams. The dirham, whose comparatively low value was better suited than the dinar for local transactions and the payment of agricultural taxes, had been an abundant coinage during the period of the cotton boom, even though silver sources dried up in the tenth/fourth century, causing many mints to put out coins alloyed with copper, bronze, and lead.[44] In his classic mint study *The Numismatic History of Rayy*, George C. Miles lists all the coins he knew of emanating from this bustling city in the vicinity of Tehran.[45] Prior to 913/301, the Rayy mint was under the control of the Abbasid caliphate in Baghdad, and its abundant issues were almost entirely silver dirhams. Once the independent Samanid dynasty based in Bukhara began minting at Rayy, however, the ratio of gold to silver among extant issues changed. Three-quarters of the Samanid issues (thirty-two out of forty-two) were gold. Then in 945/334 the Buyid dynasty took over. These rulers were based in Rayy. Being Shi'ite, they had few connections with the local Sunni governments that ruled Khurasan and Central Asia, and presumably controlled the Silk Road. The Buyid issues from the Rayy mint were over two thirds silver (forty-four out of sixty-three). The Afghanistan-based Ghaznavids came next in 1029/420 and issued two silver dirhams for every gold dinar (nine out of thirteen). Finally, after the Turkomans trounced the Ghaznavid army at Dandanqan, the Seljuqs took over the Rayy mint in 1042/434. Their issues were, for all intents and purposes, all gold dinars (forty out of forty-one). In a less comprehensive survey of coins minted in Nishapur that I carried out in 1967, I found that 10 percent of the issues of Mahmud of Ghazna were silver (fifteen out of 147), whereas under the first Seljuq sultan, Tughril Beg, silver virtually vanished (two dirhams out of 125 dinars).

Though the nature of coin collecting generally causes gold to be overrepresented in museums and private holdings, the almost total shift from ninth-/third-century silver to eleventh-/fifth-century gold is too stark to be accidental. Nor can it be ascribed to a lack of silver, because debased coins were common earlier. The shift to gold under the Seljuqs suggests instead both a move away from agricultural taxation as the regime's financial base, and a heightened interest in high-value import trading for which gold was a more useful currency than (debased) silver. Luxury consumption at court and the ease of using gold for military payrolls probably played a role as well. The new decorative art styles of the Seljuq period, such as Kashan luster ware and Minai ware featuring elaborately painted scenes, indicate consumption patterns catering more to luxury buyers than to the urban bourgeoisie of the cotton boom era.

To bring the argument of this chapter full circle, we will close with some final comments on camels. Though images of camels rarely occur in Samanid and Ghaznavid art, a recurrent motif in Seljuq pottery decoration is the image of an unridden two-humped camel, presumably part of a caravan (fig. 4.4). As already discussed, Iran was added to the domain of one-humped camel use

FIGURE 4.4.    Two-humped camels on Seljuq pottery. (By permission of the Freer Gallery of Art, Smithsonian Institution, Washington, DC.)

FIGURE 4.5.    Bahram Gur on Sasanid silver plate. (By permission of the Metropolitan
              Museum of Art.)

after the Arab conquest, or possibly a bit before in some western areas. Several
extant Sasanid or Sasanid-style silver plates show images of the Sasanid shah
Bahram Gur (Bahram V, r. 421–438) hunting on camelback with his beloved
slave girl Azada perched behind him. All the plates show one-humped camels,
usually unrealistically drawn, as do the more realistic rock reliefs showing
hunting scenes at Taq-e Bustan, a Sasanid site in northwestern Iran (fig. 4.5).
The same legendary image reappears on Seljuq ceramics, except that the camel
is by then of the two-humped variety (fig. 4.6). Still later, in the thirteenth to
fourteenth/seventh to eighth centuries, when Iran had become warm again,
Iranian artists returned to painting the scene with a very shaggy one-humped
camel that can be assumed to be a Turkoman breed (fig. 4.7). Because it is fair

FIGURE 4.6.    Bahram Gur on Seljuq period pottery. (By permission of the Metropolitan
               Museum of Art.)

to assume that the animal the artists of these different periods depicted was
the one commonly known to them, this change from one to two humps and
back again reinforces the impression given by the pictures of two-humped
caravan animals that the one-humped camel, including the hybrid *bukht*,
largely disappeared from (northern) Iran during the late Seljuq period.

So if the Oghuz, as we have argued, were indeed one-humped camel herders breeding hybrid animals for caravan work and military remounts, and if
they did migrate into Khurasan in order to save their livestock from increasingly severe winters, then their effort seems to have fallen short of full success. The one-humped beasts gradually disappeared and did not reappear

FIGURE 4.7.    Bahram Gur on tile from the Mongol period. (By permission of the Victoria and
            Albert Museum.)

until the weather became warm again. Perhaps it was this continuing livestock problem that prompted the Oghuz who relocated peacefully under
Sultan Mahmud to become marauders. And perhaps the reason they continued to head westward, as the Seljuq offer to "drive away the Iraqi . . . Turkmens" makes clear they did, reflects in part a search for still warmer pastures.[46] Whatever the case, the westward push of the Oghuz was almost
certainly responsible for the introduction of one-humped camels with thick
coats of hair into Anatolia and the establishment there of the practice of
breeding hybrids.[47] They also brought to Anatolia a fascination with "camel
wrestling," the pitting of two rutting males against each other, that shows up
down to the present day in other Turkish-speaking societies as well . . . but
not among the Arabs of Syria and Mesopotamia directly to the south.

# Chapter Five

## A MOMENT IN WORLD HISTORY

T HE RISE AND FALL OF BOURGEOIS Iranian society does not feature in anyone's narrative of world history. The closest approximation is in Richard N. Frye's book *The Golden Age of Persia*, subtitled *The Arabs in the East*.[1] But even there the seeming contradiction between the title and the subtitle epitomizes the problem of representing Iranian history in the early Islamic centuries. Should the extraordinary flourishing of Iran's highland plateau be ascribed to the Arabs who invaded or to the native Iranians? To Muslims exclusively or to the society as a whole? Is the cultural dynamism to be read only in Arabic texts or in Persian writings as well? Only in books by Muslims or also in the writings of Zoroastrians, Christians, and Jews?

The practice of historians has long been to subordinate the story of Iran in this time period to the story of Islam. The militant movement that overthrew the unimpeachably Arab caliphal dynasty of the Umayyads in 750/108 came from Iranian territory and engaged many Iranian converts to Islam in both its leadership and its soldiery. Yet it is represented primarily as a turning point in the history of Islam. The Abbasid dynasty that was the beneficiary of this movement gradually adopted many of the ceremonial, administrative, and cultural practices of the Iranian Sasanid regime that had succumbed to the Arab invaders a century earlier. Yet this is most often seen as symptomatic of Islam's capacity for absorbing and breathing new life into the traditions of its diverse peoples. The personalities, forces, and controversies that shaped the developing institutions of the Islamic religion did not just play out on the Baghdad stage, but also in burgeoning cities throughout Iran. Yet insofar as the language in which these controversies are recorded was almost exclusively Arabic, their historical moment is elided with that of the Arab Muslims whose extraordinary conquests had brought Iran into the caliphal empire.

All these representations are valid when seen through the prism of Islamic history, of course, although they are somewhat less valid as part of Arab history, because specialists on matters Arabian frequently forget to mention how many of the most prominent authors of medieval works in Arabic grew up in Persian-speaking homes. In either case, however, what is missing is any narrative of the transformation that the Iranian heartland as such underwent between 650/29 and 1000/390, or of the subsequent undoing of much of that transformation between 1000/390 and 1200/696.

A politically oriented historian might cite the lack of a centralized Iranian state, and Iran's actual incorporation in an empire centered on Iraq, as adequate explanation for this skewed perspective. After all, when the temporal power of the caliphate began to erode in the ninth/third century, several parts of Iran became wholly or partially independent under ruling houses of Iranian ethnic origin. The importance of these successor states, and of such specifically Iranian characteristics as their use of pre-Islamic symbolism and patronage of Persian-language writings, has been amply and properly recognized.[2] But because no successor state succeeded in establishing itself over most of Iran until the Oghuz Turkomans created the Seljuq sultanate in the eleventh/fifth century, the separate histories of these ethnically Iranian principalities, which were frequently at war with one another, cannot easily be summed to a history of Iran as a whole.

Although this book has concentrated on economic aspects of Iran's transformations because they are the ones that are the hardest to extract from sparse and often indirect sources, it is reasonable to close with some consideration of Iran's early Islamic history in a much broader compass, namely, its impact on world history.

Comprehensive histories of Iran through the ages lavish attention on a series of pre-Islamic empires: Achaemenids, Seleucids, Parthians, Sasanids.[3] But in every one of these instances, the capital province of the empire was Mesopotamia, usually around the Baghdad area, and the surviving political narratives provide the greatest detail in their accounts of conflicts with foes

coming from west of Mesopotamia: Greeks, Phoenicians, Romans, Byzan-
tines. Information about the Iranian plateau is rare; without archaeology almost nothing would be known. The few facts that are available, however, are
consistent with the image of a rural aristocracy living quite grandly, a village-
based grain-growing economy with very little urbanization, and a role in the
imperial polity of supplying cavalry for the armies of the kings. Oddly enough,
this description is not far from the image of Iran in the post-Seljuq period
down to around 1500/905, except for a dramatic increase in pastoral nomadism; a persistence of city life, though on a reduced scale from its heyday in the
tenth/fourth century; and the disappearance of Mesopotamia as an imperial
center to which the society of the plateau is subordinate. As the general histories make clear, the horse warriors of the Seljuq and post-Seljuq era generally fight for rulers who are based in Iran proper.

What was the impact, then, of the centuries intervening between the
fall of the Sasanids and the rise of the Seljuqs, when Iran became suddenly
transformed into one of the world's most productive and dynamic urban societies? Before addressing this question, let us take a more general look at the
transformation.

In moviemaking, a jumpcut is an abrupt, even jarring, change of scene
that sometimes makes the screenplay hard to follow. The preceding chapters have included many such abrupt jumps from one topic to another. So
now I wish to draw the assorted topics together in a more narrative vision
of Iran's economy in the early Islamic centuries, connecting the arguments
that have been advanced here with some others that I have elaborated in
earlier publications.

When the Arab invasions brought the Sasanid Empire to an end, the
invaders had no particular plan for what would come next. Different conquered areas adapted to the change of regime in different ways. In the Iranian
plateau region, the economy that the Arabs gained control of was primarily
agricultural and self-sufficient, though there was also a substantial trade,
much of it in luxury goods, along the route linking Mesopotamia with Central Asia and China. This trade was anchored by a number of small, walled
garrison towns. The fact that Arab armies campaigned as far east as Kyrgyz-
stan, more than 2000 miles from their desert homeland, while elsewhere
stabilizing their borders much closer to familiar territory, to wit, along the

Taurus Mountain frontier of southern Anatolia and at the first cataract of the Nile in Egypt, indicates that the new rulers fully understood the importance of the Silk Road trade. In all likelihood, some Arab merchants or stockbreeders even participated in the trade before the Muslims came, or they themselves became Muslims.

The conquests not only brought to power a new ruling elite, but also delivered large quantities of money into Arab hands in the form of booty, military pay, and tax revenues. Unlike Iraq, Egypt, and Tunisia, where the Arab presence was concentrated in large encampments, or Palestine and Syria, which were contiguous with traditional tribal grazing lands in the Arabian desert, Muslim rule in Iran operated through smaller army garrisons spotted at a number of strategic locales. Gorgan received more Arabs than most other places because it guarded the Karakum Desert frontier that separated Iran from the lands of the Turks to the north, and Marv received the most because it protected the Oxus as well as the Karakum frontier. Farther to the east, a large Arab garrison at Balkh anchored Muslim control in northern Afghanistan and the mountainous lands north of the Oxus. All of this before the year 750/132.

In Qom, one of the smaller Arab settlements, the question of how to adapt to life in Iran found an answer that seems to have reflected conditions in the piedmont districts more generally. Looking for a place to invest their money (my apologies for the anachronistic modern terminology), certain Arab entrepreneurs, almost certainly Yemenis by origin, hit on the idea of digging qanats and creating new villages devoted to the cultivation of cotton.

Islamic law as it crystallized in the early Abbasid period, when these villages were forming, included a "homestead" provision that granted freehold ownership to people who brought uncultivable land into production. Founding new villages in areas of desert watered by newly dug qanats thus provided an avenue for intrusive Arabs to become landowners without contesting land rights with the much more numerous Iranian landowners. The latter continued in possession of their own villages. Piedmont Iran's geography and long-established techniques of qanat excavation opened up this possibility in a way that could not easily be imitated in other conquest areas. Farther west in the Zagros Mountains, or farther east in stretches of arable land along the

Tejen, Murghab, Oxus, and Zeravshan rivers, Arab settlers seem to have found other sorts of opportunity. But the information particular to Qom is particularly revealing.

To repay the high cost of qanat and village construction, the new entrepreneurs, which included a minority of non-Muslims, planted summer crops instead of grain. Wheat and barley, the mainstay of Sasanid agriculture, were normally grown on rain-fed, spring-fed, or runoff-irrigated land that did not require so great an investment in irrigation. Pomegranates, apricots, melons, and vegetables for local consumption were appropriate for irrigated gardens close to towns, but the ideal crop for somewhat more distant villages was cotton, a plant that was unfamiliar to most Iranians but that Yemeni Arabs knew how to cultivate and process from their land of origin.

In terms of total acreage, cotton did not come close to displacing grain, but its impact transformed the nonfarming economy nevertheless. Cotton had to be freed of seeds, cleaned, combed, spun into thread, and woven into cloth. Dying, bleaching, fulling, and tailoring were also involved, depending on the fabric being produced. These industrial processes entailed a higher concentration of labor than farming villages could normally supply, and the transport and marketing of finished products similarly depended on well-developed distribution systems. Thus the emergence of cotton as an agricultural commodity provided an economic impetus for the governing points in which the Arabs had planted garrisons to expand into towns and cities.

In Sasanid times cotton farming and cotton cloth had been virtually unknown in the plateau region, although it had already been introduced into Central Asia on a fairly minor scale through contacts with India. But by the early ninth/third century cotton was already developing into the economic mainstay of an Arab-Muslim society that no longer occupied itself primarily with military operations. At the same time, cotton acquired a strong doctrinal association with Islam. Learned Muslims in Iran, a large proportion of whom, apparently around 40 percent, were engaged in or funded from one or another aspect of cotton production, popularized antisilk, pro-cotton teachings. Some of these prescriptive *hadith* they traced directly to Muhammad and others to early Arab responses to encounters with the defeated Sasanid elite. Religious precepts thus encouraged a rapid growth in cotton consumption as new converts to Islam sought to emulate the flowing, plain-cloth style of dress of the Arabs and the earliest converts. Sasanid-era silk brocades remained popular among the elite strata of the majority non-Muslim population. Silk also came into fashion among the Muslim civil elite, particularly in Baghdad; but the religious prohibitions were honored nevertheless through the government's establishment of *tiraz* factories. The cotton (and in Egypt, linen) fabrics produced in these factories for fabrication into robes of honor made explicit the connection between Islam and textile preferences.

A visible competition arose between a Muslim lifestyle and a non-Muslim lifestyle, particularly in the growing cities. This was manifested not just in clothing preferences, but also in ceramics. Muslim austerity and reverence for the Arabic script contrasted dramatically with Sasanid luxury and figurative ornamentation. Cotton probably also contributed to the spread of Islam through the farmers attracted to work in the new cotton villages being classified as Muslims, regardless of their private convictions or depth of knowledge of the Muslim faith.

The differential between tax rates on grain and on cotton shows that growing cotton was highly profitable. The fact that Iraq was geographically unsuited to growing cotton enhanced this profitability because Arabs and new converts there consumed cloth imported from Iran. The cotton boom fueled exuberant growth in the size of Iran's cities during the ninth/third and tenth/fourth centuries. It provided money for urban construction and land speculation; it provided employment in textile manufacturing; and it encouraged new converts to migrate to the cities and share in the Islam-focused prosperity. Never before had a domestically produced industrial commodity played such an important role in the overall Iranian economy, or competed in importance with the products carried by Silk Road caravans.

The scholarly elite (ulama) of the Muslim community, through their religious endorsement of cotton consumption and deep involvement in its production, stood at the center of urbanization and commerce. Through their own enterprise or through intermarriage, the most illustrious scholarly lineages had acquired, by the late tenth/fourth century, such significant commercial and landowning interests that they constituted a patrician class that dominated local urban society and politics, more on the pattern of the urban elites of late medieval Europe than of the earlier, legally defined Roman patricians. To be sure, many ulama families had commercial interests other than, or in addition to, cotton; but the wearing of plain white cotton (or linen) became the hallmark of the religious profession, and continues to be so to the present day.

A biographical note about an eminent scholar from Gorgan epitomizes this development. After praising Abu Sa'd al-Isma'ili (d. 1007/397) for his erudition in Arabic and Islamic law, his piety, and his generosity, the biographer writes:

> Among those things by which God blessed him was that when his death drew near, all of what he possessed by way of wealth and estates departed him. He had sent cotton to Bab al-Abwab [Derbent on the western side of the Caspian Sea]; it was all lost at sea. He had goods that were being transported from Isfahan; Kurds descended upon them and took them. He had some wheat being shipped to him from Khurasan; a group of people fell upon it and plundered it. He had an estate in the village known as Kuskara; Qabus ibn Washmagir [Gorgan's ruler at that time] ordered that its trees be uprooted, and they were. The qanat was filled in and all his property seized.[4]

Iran's creative urban culture continued to expand even as the cotton boom waned in the tenth/fourth century. Centuries-old traditions do not easily pass away, and the landowning families that joined the Muslim community in great numbers in the late ninth/third and early tenth/fourth centuries saw no reason to ape the Arabs just because Muhammad happened to have been born in Mecca. By this time the caliphate had lost political control, and local rulers of Iranian descent had taken power in most parts of Iran. With them, pre-Islamic styles and tastes reappeared, and the Persian language enjoyed a literary revival. In the cities, society became more complex. Some patrician families retained attitudes rooted in earlier, Arab-centered, Muslim practice; others favored newer attitudes and practices that were more responsive to the indigenous Iranian population, and more welcoming to new converts. This division contributed to a growing current of factional conflict even though the nominal basis of the conflict was differing (Sunni) views on Islamic law.

Cotton continued to be a mainstay of the manufacturing and export economy, but among the civil elite it had certainly lost its cachet as a preferred clothing textile by the mid-tenth/fourth century. At the same time, city growth through rural–urban migration, partly prompted by conversion and partly by economic opportunity, was reaching a point where the surplus food production of the labor-starved countryside was barely enough to sustain the populations of nonproductive urbanites. In some regions, such as the area around Nishapur in Khurasan, the percentage of the population living in the ten largest cities became comparable to the rate found in northern Italy and Flanders, the most highly urbanized parts of Europe. Unlike their European counterparts, however, Iran's plateau cities did not have the benefit of inexpensive water transport for bringing foodstuffs from distant growing regions.[5] Instances of drought and crop failure thus became increasingly perilous, leading governments to lower the tax rates on wheat and barley in an effort to sustain the necessary level of food production. A likely consequence would have been a partial shift from cotton to grain farming. This in turn would have touched the economic life of the cities by reducing the volume of cotton manufactures and exports.

Though a string of bad winters in the first half of the tenth/fourth century gave northern Iran a taste of what a major change in the weather might bring, the Big Chill did not set in until the eleventh/fifth century. By that time the bourgeois life-style fostered in large part by the cotton boom, and manifested in the social dominance of the patrician class, was already showing signs of stress. Factional feuding along religious lines had become endemic, and leading patrician families were sometimes bitterly at odds with one another. Episodes of famine and disease seem to have become more numerous, but the historical narratives are too spotty to be sure that this was the case.

The narratives more reliably inform us of an unprecedented movement of the Oghuz Turkomans from Central Asia into Iran. Though the stereotype of Central Asian nomadic society focuses on horse herding, the tribes that entered Khurasan at this time herded both horses and one-humped camels. Being essential for military purposes, the former probably outnumbered the latter. But the camels provided an important economic link with the caravan trade along the Silk Road. The Oghuz pastoralists interbred their one-humped females with two-humped males to produce unusually large and strong animals that were ideal for carrying loads or, in the case of females, for soldiers riding through desert terrain. The traditional lands of the Oghuz were located in the northern reaches of the Karakum Desert. The new lands they sought in their migrations were on the considerably warmer southern fringe of the same desert.

Exactly why the Turkomans were allowed to enter Khurasan is unclear, but Sultan Mahmud of Ghazna, who authorized their relocation, probably assumed that they would fit reasonably well into the economy as producers of valuable livestock. On the Oghuz side, the cooling of the climate must have enhanced their desire to relocate, if it was not the sole rationale, because their one-humped camels had a hard time surviving cold winters. As it turned out, these first Turkoman immigrants turned to pillaging, and some were driven away by the Ghaznavid army. Continuing livestock problems may well have contributed to this, because, instead of returning to Central Asia or moving back north to Khwarazm, many made their marauding way deeper into Iran. Ultimately, they found their way to Anatolia.

The next wave of Oghuz also petitioned to move from the northern Karakum to the warmer southern side of the desert, so it is likely that if the first wave had been experiencing livestock problems, the second wave was too. Fearing a repetition of the pillaging carried out by the earlier migrants, Sultan Mahmud's son Masʿud forced the new group, led by the Seljuq family, into a military confrontation. Sultan Masʿud lost the crucial battle of Dandanqan and ceded Khurasan to the Seljuqs.

Unlike the Oghuz who had preceded them, or the Oghuz who ravaged Khurasan more than a century later after inflicting a surprise defeat on Sultan Sanjar, the last powerful Seljuq ruler, in 1153/547, the tribespeople that the Seljuqs led into Khurasan remained disciplined and helped the new rulers build a unified and comparatively peaceful domain extending from Iraq to northern Afghanistan. As for the economy, the noted historian Anne Lambton has written: "The Saljuq invasion does not appear to have caused a major break in the general continuity of rural prosperity."[6] However, the supporting evidence cited in her accompanying discussion mostly concerns southern Iran, which was less affected by the Big Chill. Khurasan, she admits, declined significantly in importance. Seljuq land policies featured increased reliance on land grants (*iqta'*) in return for military or government service. This may have temporarily raised revenues by giving the grantees license to oppress the peasantry, but it would have done nothing to restore flagging production in areas facing environmental deterioration. Nor is it likely to have encouraged landowners to invest more in their properties.

The superior leadership of the Seljuq family probably stemmed from prior involvement with caravan trading along the Silk Road. Like the Mongols of the thirteenth/seventh century, the Seljuqs focused their economic attention on long-distance trade. Among other effects, this served to popularize artistic styles and techniques derived from Chinese models and to encourage the growth of luxury consumption in ruling circles.

The undeniable prosperity of early Seljuq times could not conceal the fact that the agricultural infrastructure of northern Iran was suffering badly from nomadic incursions, rural insecurity, government neglect, and (especially) the Big Chill. Most cities suffered severe factional discord. The factional enmity dated from the tenth/fourth century, but its increasingly violent manifestations bespeak a competition for material resources that were becoming increasingly scarce and unreliable.

By the early twelfth/sixth century, northern Iran was in a declining condition. Members of patrician families that had the necessary financial means and scholarly connections outside Iran migrated to Iraq, Syria, Anatolia, or India. The patrician-dominated bourgeois market that had shaped consumption in pre-Seljuq times faded away, and Iran entered a long period of minimal contribution to the religious culture of Islam. The inability of the Khwarazmshahs to restore prosperity and order after Sanjar's reign highlights the degree of damage Iran suffered during the Big Chill. By then warmth had returned, but Iran's human and economic resources were too depleted to permit any significant recovery before the Mongol onslaught.

On a world scale, Iran's moment of efflorescence had five significant impacts that have no parallel in earlier or later Iranian history. First, Mesopotamia under the Abbasid caliphs became the center of a vast and balanced economic region stretching from Central Asia to Tunisia instead of the eastern border of the lands around the Mediterranean. The wealth in silver dirhams derived from taxation and commerce in the lands to the east of the Zagros mountains exceeeded the wealth in gold dinars derived from the older urbanized economies of Syria, Palestine, Egypt, and North Africa. Where the various pre-Islamic dynasties that ruled from Mesopotamia between 500 BCE and the beginning of the Arab conquests had repeatedly sought to expand westward, the Muslim state paid much greater attention to eastern affairs. Abbasid caliphs rarely set foot in Egypt, Palestine, or coastal Syria; and Tunisia was the first province to be granted autonomy—in return for an annual tribute payment—by the Baghdad caliphs shortly after the year 800/183. By contrast, the first ten Abbasid rulers were all deeply involved in military campaigns or political machinations on the Iranian plateau, and several of them (e.g., al-Mahdi, Harun al-Rashid, al-Ma'mun, and al-Mu'tasim) spent substantial amounts of time there.

. One reflection of this eastern orientation was a change in the locus of trading momentum. The Silk Road had always found its primary western terminus in one of a series of Mesopotamian capitals from Babylon to Ctesiphon that were built near the point where the Tigris and Euphrates rivers flow nearest to one another. Baghdad proved to be the last of these. But under earlier dynasties, substantial quantities of Silk Road goods had moved on up the Euphrates by caravan to find their way into Mediterranean commerce, usually being sold at entrepots like Dura Europus or Palmyra located near the frontier between the state based in Mesopotamia and some rival to the west. The early Islamic centuries, however, saw no great trading centers in those areas, nor does it appear that merchants in Syria, Egypt, or Byzantine Anatolia traded very extensively with Baghdad. It seems, rather, that the growing prosperity of urban Iran created an expanded outlet for Silk Road commodities that in earlier centuries had simply transited across northern Iran by caravan without being subject to much market activity at intermediate points. The upshot of this development is that the preferences and styles of the people living in the cities on the Iranian plateau region became defining components of the emergent Abbasid culture of Islam.

Second, Egypt, Palestine, and Syria were so overshadowed by Iran that they hold a comparatively negligible place in the history of the Middle East between 750/132 and 1100/493. This had never happened since the advent of the pharaohs, and it was not to happen after the undermining of the Iranian economy by the Big Chill allowed the coastlands of the Mediterranean to resume the paramount role in the Middle East that they continue to play to the present day. It is symptomatic of this diminished status that the only truly important Muslim political phenomenon at the eastern end of the Mediterranean after 750/132, the rise and fall of the Fatimid state in Tunisia, Egypt, and coastal Syria between 909/296 and 1171/566, defined itself in opposition to Abbasid Baghdad, both politically and doctrinally, but never acquired the power to mount a credible military challenge.

Another sort of evidence comes from a tally of geographically specific names in comprehensive biographical dictionaries of Islamic religious scholars. Between 743/125 and 1179/575, the proportion of notable scholars from Egypt and Syria/Palestine combined never exceeds 20 percent. Then it suddenly shoots up to a dominant position. By contrast, the proportion of scholars from Iran alone never falls below 30 percent between 840/225 and 1131/525. Then it tumbles (see Table 5.1).

How different medieval Mediterranean history might have been if Baghdad's rulers, and their local successors in various parts of Iran, had cared about what happened in the west. Spain went its separate way. Tunisia's conquest of Sicily did not interest people in the east. The Fatimid takeover of Tunisia, Algeria, and Morocco was a distant event of little note until the new Isma'ili Shi'ite countercaliphate successfully expanded into Egypt and parts of Syria. And even then, the Isma'ilis in Iran—the Assassins—loomed as a more potent threat in the imaginations of men of affairs in Mesopotamia and Iran.

Would greater attention to the affairs of Muslims living to the west of the Syrian–Iraqi desert have meant a stronger, more coordinated, and more aggressive attitude toward Christian Europe? Would it have enlivened Mediterranean trade? Would it have enhanced Europe's awareness of and concerns about Islam? There is no way of telling. But it is strikingly apparent that the eleventh/fifth century, when climate change triggered widespread economic difficulty in Iran accompanied by nomadization, urban decline, and the emigration of the learned elite, also saw a marked revival of economic, cultural, and political interaction among the various Muslim and Christian principalities bordering on the Mediterranean. It is not inconceivable that the

TABLE 5.1  Regional Representation among Muslim Religious Scholars

| DATES | TOTAL | IRAN | IRAQ | EG | SYR | EG+SY | OTHER |
|---|---|---|---|---|---|---|---|
| 709/91 | 161 | 9% | 46% | 6% | 12% | 18% | 27% |
| 734/116 | 180 | 8% | 61% | 4% | 13% | 17% | 14% |
| 758/141 | 199 | 12% | 62% | 6% | 12% | 18% | 8% |
| 782/166 | 213 | 24% | 54% | 4% | 10% | 14% | 8% |
| 806/191 | 133 | 38% | 39% | 6% | 13% | 19% | 4% |
| 831/216 | 136 | 32% | 48% | 7% | 4% | 11% | 9% |
| 855/241 | 186 | 38% | 39% | 4% | 10% | 14% | 8% |
| 879/266 | 185 | 37% | 39% | 5% | 12% | 17% | 7% |
| 903/291 | 184 | 40% | 36% | 3% | 10% | 13% | 11% |
| 928/316 | 173 | 36% | 42% | 6% | 8% | 14% | 8% |
| 952/341 | 168 | 41% | 32% | 5% | 10% | 15% | 12% |
| 976/366 | 144 | 39% | 31% | 7% | 12% | 19% | 11% |
| 1000/391 | 123 | 51% | 22% | 4% | 10% | 14% | 13% |
| 1025/416 | 154 | 49% | 29% | 3% | 6% | 9% | 13% |
| 1049/441 | 127 | 39% | 34% | 4% | 8% | 12% | 15% |
| 1073/466 | 159 | 36% | 33% | 4% | 11% | 15% | 16% |
| 1097/491 | 151 | 32% | 32% | 5% | 15% | 20% | 16% |
| 1122/516 | 189 | 23% | 37% | 6% | 20% | 26% | 14% |
| 1146/541 | 193 | 23% | 39% | 7% | 19% | 26% | 11% |
| 1170/566 | 228 | 14% | 29% | 9% | 38% | 47% | 10% |
| 1194/591 | 192 | 6% | 17% | 11% | 49% | 60% | 17% |
| 1219/616 | 219 | 8% | 12% | 10% | 60% | 70% | 10% |

Mediterranean revival depended in some measure on the waning of Iran's dynamism.

The third broad impact of Iran's moment in the sun was that it forever changed the template of life on the plateau. Though nomads would from time to time ravage the land and bring down ruling dynasts, the idea of Iran as a land of cities persisted. Even when landowners enjoying royal favor came to control scores of villages, the pre-Islamic pattern of a warrior aristocracy settled in a dispersed fashion throughout the countryside never returned. The new landowners either were tribal chieftains, in which case they might indeed live

in the country, but as pastoralists, or chose to live in or near town and send
their agents to collect rents from their villages. To this day Iranians identify
themselves by the urban center of the region they come from and by its traditional customs and local manufactures. They are Rashti or Shirazi or Tabrizi.
Without the urbanization of the ninth/third and tenth/fourth centuries,
this pattern would not have been there to guide the country's recovery in the
fifteenth/ninth century after a century of Mongol rule and the renewed dis-
ruptions of the Timurid era.

Language is the fourth area of impact. Every historian of Iran and of Islam has speculated on the reason or reasons for the failure of Arabic to
achieve the dominance in Iran that it gained in the other regions conquered
in the initial Islamic conquests. New Persian, a streamlined koine written in
Arabic script, first appeared during the period of Iran's economic boom; and
great works of literature were already being authored in this language by the
time the Big Chill set in in the eleventh/fifth century. This did not mean,
however, that the several Middle Iranian languages of preconquest times—
Middle Persian, Parthian, Sogdian, Bactrian, Khwarazmian, and so on—
promptly disappeared. Indeed, Yaghnobi, a modern descendant of Sogdian,
is still spoken in parts of Tajikistan. So not only was New Persian distinctive
in its use of the Arabic script, but it saturated and lent linguistic uniformity
to an Iranian language zone that had previously been multilingual and politically divided among a number of principalities.

Religion, as symbolized by the Arabic script, is the ostensible common
denominator underlying this newfound linguistic uniformity. Zoroastrians
continued to write religious books in Middle Persian. But to the degree that
Islam had anything to say doctrinally about language, it favored Arabic, the
language of the Qur'an. Moreover, the religious elite of the Muslim community preferred for many generations to write in Arabic, leaving New Persian,
at least initially, to the poets, storytellers, and historians. References to Islam
or its teachings are uncommon in the corpus of early compositions in New
Persian. However, that corpus is quite small and consists mostly of poems
and romances before the tenth/fourth century.

An alternative common denominator could be the urban-based economic linkages that grew out of the cotton boom that began at the beginning of the ninth/third century. Muslims played the dominant role in build-

ing the new economy and populating the growing cities. They also became the most active participants in overland trade as they transported cotton cloth (and other goods) from as far east as Samarqand toward the great consumption center of Baghdad. New Persian, therefore, may have arisen the way Swahili and Bahasa Indonesia did in later periods of Islamic history, namely, as the language of merchants who resorted to a simplified grammar and morphology to gloss over the differences among the Middle Iranian tongues used in various localities, and who found an easy way to incorporate Arabic loan words by adopting the Arabic script. Known to all literate Muslims, but probably not to most non-Muslim Iranians, the Arabic script would similarly have afforded a means of overriding the preceding diversity of Middle Iranian writing systems.

Looking at the innovators of New Persian as a newly rising class of Muslim merchants and manufacturers responding to a pressing need to communicate with their counterparts in other parts of the Iranian cultural zone would help explain the uniformity, simplicity, and broad geographical extent of the new tongue. And it would raise the possibility that the Arabic script was deliberately intended to define a specifically Muslim commercial and cultural network. However, linking the emergence of New Persian to the cotton boom is entirely speculative. No commercial writings have survived from the period in any language, and the number of Iranian poets known to have written in Arabic dwarfs the handful who experimented with Persian.

By contrast, linking the decline of the Iranian agricultural economy in the era of the Big Chill to the spread outside Iran of New Persian is fairly obvious. No New Persian authors are known to have worked outside Iran before the Seljuq period, but by the thirteenth/seventh century both Anatolia and India were known for the exquisite Persian verses composed there by Jalal al-Din Rumi (d. 1273/671) and Amir Khusraw (d. 1325/725), respectively. What is important about these master poets for present purposes is not their personal lives but the fact that they rhapsodized for Persian-speaking audiences and had Persian-speaking colleagues and imitators in these foreign lands. So far as is known, the pre-Islamic Iranian dynasties never exported their languages to other lands. Not even to Mesopotamia, which was under Iranian rule for most of the millennium preceding the Arab conquests. What supported the spread of New Persian from the Seljuq era onward was not just the military success of the Turkoman warriors in Anatolia and Afghan tribesmen in northern India, but the migration out of Iran of literate scholars and litterateurs relocating themselves in response to deteriorating conditions in their homeland. To be sure, the Mongol invasion in the early thirteenth/seventh century put a capstone on Iran's decline and forced many people to flee the destruction of their cities and not just the freezing of their crops. But there is ample evidence that the Iranian diaspora was well under way before the Mongols arrived. And there is similarly ample evidence that the emergence of New Persian as a cosmopolitan language of administration and culture from the Bay of Bengal to the Aegean Sea left a telling mark on world history.

The fifth and final impact of Iran's boom and bust lies in the area of religion. In the sixteenth/tenth century, under the aegis of the Safavid dynasty, Iran became both declaratively and practically a Shi'ite land. Scholars disagree about how well implanted in the country Shi'ism was before the advent of the Safavids and on the extent of the coerced conversions that took place once the new identity was declared. All agree, however, that the interposition of a Shi'ite Iran between a Sunni Ottoman state to the west, a Sunni Uzbek state to the northeast, and a predominantly Sunni Muslim presence in India to the southeast powerfully shaped the history of the Muslim world from that time until the present.

From the ninth/third through the eleventh/fifth century, on the other hand, Iran was a predominantly Sunni land. To be sure, there are many indications that Shi'ites constituted a strong presence from time to time. The Buyid dynasty, for example, adhered first to the Zaidi and then to the Imami form of Shi'ism. And the Isma'ili movement attracted many believers, particularly in the time of the Big Chill. Nevertheless, any tally of writers, thinkers, and religious leaders for the period of rapid urbanization and the cotton boom will come up with vastly more Sunnis than Shi'ites. Shi'ite ulama composed their own lists of leading scholars, but the city-based biographical dictionaries that have played such an important role in the arguments of this book are almost entirely Sunni and much more extensive than any Shi'ite compilation. Moreover, as table 5.1 shows, the Sunni intellectual output of Iran overshadowed almost every other region of the caliphate during the boom period. Although Ibn al-'Imad, whose biographical compilation provided the data for the table (see the earlier discussion of table 4.1), was himself a Syrian, the combined share of Islamic scholarship apportionable to Egypt and Syria combined never exceeds 20 percent before the late Seljuq period

The elite emigration that took place from the late eleventh/fifth century onward effectively stripped the Sunni mass of the population of its religious leadership while at the same time the factional discord and shrinking subsistence base of the cities in the north destroyed many of the mosques and seminaries (madrasas) that had nurtured that leadership. The madrasa as a dedicated center for higher religious education had originated in Iran in the tenth/fourth century, if not before, and the institution had spread throughout the country before migrating into non-Iranian lands, more often than not with Iranian professors as inaugural academic directors. But by the beginning of the thirteenth/seventh century few noteworthy seminaries were still functioning, particularly in comparison with the many that were then flourishing in Iraq, Syria, Egypt, and elsewhere.

It could be argued, of course, that the famously destructive onslaught of the Mongols would have wiped out Iran's Sunni religious leadership even if it had not become depleted before Genghiz Khan's first invasion in 1218/614. But this would make it difficult to account for the strong persistence of Sunni Islam in Central Asia, where the Mongol domination lasted even longer. It seems, rather, that the economically induced erosion of the Sunni spiritual leadership left Iran open to the much more populist and less legalistic guidance of Sufis, prominent members of the family of Ali, and Shiʿite preachers who ascribed divinely ordained leadership to that family. In other words, the rise of Iranian Shiʿism was facilitated, though not caused, by the collapse of what had once been a powerful, wealthy, and highly institutionalized Sunni religious establishment.

The study of world history over the past thirty years has looked with favor upon Fernand Braudel's threefold division of time and causation: "Events" are the happenings of any given moment and should not normally command the close attention of scholars interested in the grand sweep of history. "Conjunctures" occur when various forces and institutions come together in an often complex fashion to shape a new historical tendency over a period of decades or more. And the "*longue durée*" involves trends that are so drawn out chronologically as to be largely unnoticed at the time even though they can have a profound impact that lasts for centuries. Narratives concentrating on the last two of these historical dimensions commonly strive to look beyond traditional political boundaries and dynastic eras.

The idea of a "moment" in world history elides these three dimensions. It concentrates on a particular place, the Iranian plateau, at a particular time, the ninth/third through twelfth/sixth centuries. Some of its arguments deal with humdrum events: the decisions made by agricultural entrepreneurs to invest in irrigation and grow cotton; or the decisions made by camel breeders to move their livestock to warmer pastures even in the face of military opposition. Other arguments are more conjunctural: the intersecting of religious teachings, economic benefit, and symbolic assertion of Muslim supremacy in the development of an urban-based cotton industry; or the coming together of agricultural decline, nomadization of the countryside, and urban factional discord to prompt a far-reaching diaspora of Iran's religious and intellectual elite. Still others relate to the "*longue durée*," notably the hypothesis that the northern Middle East experienced a Big Chill that lasted for more than a century.

From a world historical perspective, the impact of this moment was both complex and longlasting. But the story told here has been primarily the story of Iran in an era that is commonly given short shrift by historians. The economic and cultural efflorescence fostered by cotton production and rapid urbanization on the Iranian plateau in the first three Islamic centuries differed profoundly from anything that had happened in Iran before. And even though a change in climate brought an end to Iran's agricultural prosperity and exuberant urban society, the traces of what the Iranians had created spread far and wide, and the land itself was left with a memory and a template of urban life that served as a base for revival in later and more propitious times. It was a moment to remember.

# *Notes*

### PREFACE

1. Neville Brown, *History and Climate Change* (London: Routledge, 2007), 111.

2. Personal communication, 1973. This was a subject of intense interest for Professor Ashtor, who was then a leading economic historian of medieval Islam.

3. Marshall G. S. Hodgson, *The Venture of Islam,* vol. 3 (Chicago: University of Chicago Press, 1975), 5–6.

4. Georg Wilhelm Friedrich Hegel, *The Philosophy of History* (London: The Colonial Press, 1900), 67.

5. See Chapter 2, "The Hero as Prophet. Mahomet: Islam," available as an etext at www .guttenberg.org.

### CHAPTER 1. HOW TO IDENTIFY A COTTON BOOM

1. All dates will be given in double form with the date of the Common Era preceding the Hijri date.

2. Hayyim J. Cohen, "The Economic Background and the Secular Occupations of Muslim Jurisprudents and Traditionists in the Classical Period of Islam," *Journal of the Economic and Social History of the Orient* 13, no. 1 (1970): 16–71.

3. Al-Hakim al-Naisaburi, "Ta'rikh Naisabur," facsimile ms contained in Richard N. Frye, ed., *The Histories of Nishapur* (Cambridge, MA: Harvard University Press, 1965). Though Cohen uses death dates to determine which century to assign each biographical entry to, I have deducted twenty years from the death dates in making my own calculations. The purpose of this reduction is to approximate the time period during which the subject of a biography was actually practicing his trade.

4. Richard W. Bulliet, "Medieval Nishapur: A Topographic and Demographic Reconstruction," *Studia Iranica* V (1976): 67–89.

5. Cohen, "Economic Background," 27.

6. Chapter 6 of Andrew Watson's *Agricultural Innovation in the Early Islamic World: The Diffusion of Crops and Farming Techniques, 700–1100* (Cambridge: Cambridge University Press, 1983) provides a wealth of information about the earliest history of cotton production. However, although he acknowledges the widespread diffusion of cotton growing during the Islamic period, Watson does not mention Sasanid Iran or the earliest cultivation of cotton there. For another comprehensive view of the history of cotton focusing on the Roman Empire, see Maureen Fennell Mazzaoui, *The Italian Cotton Industry in the Later Middle Ages, 1100–1600* (Cambridge: Cambridge University Press, 1981).

7. *Islamic Textiles* (London: British Museum Press, 1995), 23. Baker cites no evidence in support of her statement.

8. *The Cambridge History of Iran*, vol. 3(2), *The Seleucid, Parthian, and Sasanian Periods* (Cambridge: Cambridge University Press, 1983), 1107.

9. Mazzaoui, *Italian Cotton Industry*, 10–11.

10. Thomas Allsen, *Commodity and Exchange in the Mongol Empire: A Cultural History of Islamic Textiles* (Cambridge: Cambridge University Press, 1997), 68.

11. Liu Bo, *The Sogdian Letters from Dunhuang and the Sogdians in Dunhuang and Guzang During the Jin Dynasties* [in Chinese, 1995], 152–53, cited in Étienne de la Vaissière, *Sogdian Traders: A History*, tr. James Ward (Leiden: Brill, 2005), 52, n. 20.

12. *Sogdian Traders*, 67–69.

13. Simone-Christiane Raschmann, *Baumwolle im türkischen Zentralasien* (Wiesbaden: Harrassowitz, 1995), 17.

14. Liu Xinru, *Silk and Religion: An Exploration of Material Life and the Thought of People, AD 600–1200* (Delhi: Oxford University Press, 1996).

15. The Sanskrit word also shows up in Hebrew *karpas*, Greek *karpasos*, and Latin *carbasus*. (Mazzaoui, *Italian Cotton Industry*, 9), but it loses its specific denotation as cotton, meaning sometimes fine linen or fine wool. (Gilad J. Gevaryahu and Michael L. Wise, "Why Does the Seder Begin with *Karpas?" Jewish Bible Quarterly* 27, no. 2 (1999): 104–109). In all likelihood this philological confusion reflects Hellenistic era imports of fine textiles from India rather than an extension of cotton as a cultivar.

16. Mazzaoui (*Italian Cotton Industry*, 15) writes: "In the Roman period the crop, introduced from India and/or Turkestan, was grown on irrigated land in Iran, Babylonia, Palestine and most probably Asia Minor. . . . This early crop migration via Iran has left a firm imprint on the linguistic record. The low Latin term for cotton, *bambacium*, is borrowed from the middle Persian *pambak*. [Modern Persian is *pambeh*—RWB] In eastern Europe and Anatolia the Persian root has been preserved in the Croatian *bambák*, the Russian *bumága*, the Turkish *pamuk*, and the Hungarian *pamut*." Since Iranian traders along the Euphrates frontier would have been the conduits for cotton cloth reaching Roman lands, it is not surprising that the middle Persian word, along with the Sanskrit word, came with it. However, this does not constitute evidence for cotton being cultivated in any particular part of the Sasanid realm.

17. Watson, *Agricultural Innovation*, Part 4.

18. Richard W. Bulliet, *Conversion to Islam in the Medieval Period: An Essay in Quantitative History* (Cambridge, MA: Harvard University Press, 1979); and *Islam: The View from the Edge* (New York: Columbia University Press, 1994).

19. The paucity of data cited for Iran is strikingly evident in Eliyahu Ashtor, *Histoire des prix et des salaires dans l'Orient médiéval* (Paris: SEVPEN, 1969).

20. For Iran these matters are spelled out in Willem Floor, *Agriculture in Qajar Iran*. (Washington, DC: Mage, 2003), ch. 17.

21. For a detailed discussion of these processes, including preparation of yarn, bleaching, and dyeing, see Mazzaoui, *Italian Cotton Industry*, 74–76.

22. Pierre Briant, ed., *Irrigation et drainage dans l'antiquité*, qanats *et canalisations souterraines en Iran, en Égypte et en Grèce* (Paris: Thotm éditions, 2001), contains several articles that touch on the age of qanats. The case for a minimal early use of qanats, or possibly no pre-Islamic use at all, is made by Rémy Boucharlat in his contribution on "Les galléries de captage dans la péninsule d'Oman au premier millénaire avant J.-C." (157–84), most vividly when he quotes approvingly the remark of Peter Christensen: "I am not aware of a single case where *qanat* have been dated back to pre-historical times with any reasonable degree of certainty on the sole basis of archaeological criteria" (177–78). Briant's own contribution, however, "Retour à Polybe: *hyponomoi* et *phreatiai*" (15–40), makes an irrefutable case for the technology being known by the end of the Achaemenid era.

23. For a thorough discussion of all aspects of the silk trade see Liu Xinru, *Silk and Religion*. The author's exclusive focus on silk leaves in question the balance between silk and other textiles. See also *Cambridge History of Iran*, vol. 3, 1107–12.

24. On the survival of the regional barons see Parvaneh Pourshariati, *Decline and Fall of the Sasanian Empire: The Sasanian-Parthian Confederacy and the Arab Conquest of Iran*. (London: I.B. Tauris, 2008).

25. See, for example, George Stewart, *Names on the Land* (New York: Random House, 1945).

26. Joseph E. Schwartzberg, ed., *A Historical Atlas of South Asia* (Chicago: University of Chicago Press, 1978).

27. For examples of sale documents see Hashem Rajabzade and Kenji Eura, eds., *Sixty Persian Documents of the Qajar Period*, "Persian Documents," Series No. 32 (Tokyo: Institute for the Study of Languages and Cultures of Asia and Africa, 1999).

28. Mohammad al-Karagi, *La civilisation des eaux cachées: traité de l'exploitation des eaux souterraines*, ed. and tr. Aly Mazaheri (Nice: Université de Nice, Institut d'Études et de Recherches Interéthniqes et Interculturelles, 1973), 5.

29. *Encyclopaedia Iranica*, ed. Ehsan Yarshater, vol. 1 (London: Routledge & Kegan Paul, 1985), 57. Bibliographical references in the original are retained to demonstrate the scholarly basis of Ashraf's analysis.

30. A good account of traditional qanat construction and its complications is contained in Anthony Smith, *Blind White Fish in Persia* (New York: E. P. Dutton, 1953), 79–82, 97–100.

"Qanat Irrigation Systems: An Ancient Water Distribution System Allowing Specialized and Diverse Cropping in Desert Regions of Iran" (Islamic Republic of Iran: Centre for Sustainable Development [CENESTA], 2003) is a detailed study of every aspect of contemporary qanat usage in the area of Kashan, a city between Qom and Isfahan. The full text is available on-line at: www.cenesta.org/projects/qanat/Qanat%20Irrigation%20Systems.doc

31. Muhammad b. al-Hasan al-Hasib al-Karkhi, *Kitab inbat al-miyah al-khaffiya* (Heydarabad: Da'irat al-Maʿarif al-ʿUthmaniya, 1359 [1940]). It is generally recognized that the name *al-Karkhi*, referring to a neighborhood in Baghdad, is a corruption of *al-Karaji*, referring to the town of Karaj in the piedmont region of the Iranian plateau. In his better-known works, al-Karaji made significant advances in the field of algebra. I wish to thank Abigail Schade for bringing this text to my attention.

32. A. Ben Shemesh, tr., *Taxation in Islam*, vol. 1, *Yahya ben Adam's* Kitab al-Kharaj (Leiden: E.J. Brill, 1967), 65ff.

33. For a full discussion see Briant, "Retour à Polybe: *hyponomoi* et *phreatiai*.."

34. Javad Safinezhad, *Boneh* (Tehran: Bakhsh-e Tahqiqat-e Insan Shenasi, Mu'assaseh-ye Motalaʿat va Tahqiqat Ijtimaʿi, Daneshgah-Tehran, 1350 [1973]).

35. Javad Safinezhad, "The Climate of Iran and the Emergence of Traditional Collective Production Systems," unpublished article, 1977, map 7.

36. Ann K.S. Lambton, "An Account of the *Tarikhi Qumm*," *Bulletin of the School of Oriental and African Studies* 12, no.3–4 (1948): 586–96; and "Qum: The Evolution of a Medieval City," *Journal of the American Oriental Society* (1990): 322–39.

37. Andreas Drechsler, *Geschichte der Stadt Qom im Mittelalter* (Berlin: Klaus Schwarz Verlag, 1999).

38. Michael G. Morony, "The Age of Conversions: A Reassessment," in Michael Gervers and Ramzi J. Bikhazi, eds., *Conversion and Continuity: Indigenous Christian Communities in Islamic Lands, Eighth to Eighteenth Centuries* (Toronto: Pontifical Institute of Medieval Studies, 1990), 135–50.

39. Bulliet, *Conversion*, 44.

40. Bulliet, *Conversion*, 66–71.

41. On the personalities associated with these names see Andrew J. Newman, *The Formative Period of Twelver Shi'ism: Hadith as Discourse Between Qum and Baghdad* (London: Routledge Curzon, 2000), 38–41.

42. Lambton, "Account," 592.

43. Bulliet, *View from the Edge*, ch. 4.

44. Bulliet, *View from the Edge*, ch. 8.

45. Rudi Matthee, *The Pursuit of Pleasure: Drugs and Stimulants in Iranian History, 1500–1900* (Princeton: Princeton University Press, 2005), 217.

46. Ibn Hawqal, *Configuration*, 297.

47. Lambton, "Account," 588.

48. Smith, *White Fish*, 79–82.

49. See examples in Richard W. Bulliet, *The Patricians of Nishapur: A Study in Medieval Islamic Social History* (Cambridge, MA: Harvard University Press, 1972), Part 2 passim.

50. Cotton is included among the taxes in kind sent to Baghdad from the Caspian coast as early as the caliphate of the Abbasid al-Mansur (754–775/136–158), but the abundant water and torrid summers of that region presented a very different agricultural situation from that on the plateau (Liu, *Silk*, 152).

### CHAPTER 2. ISLAM AND COTTON

1. The data in table 2.1 come from the following biographical dictionaries: Isfahan—Abu Nuʿaim al-Isfahani, *Kitab dhikr akhbar Isbahan*, ed. S. Dedering (Leiden: E.J. Brill, 1931), 34, 2 v. Nishapur—Al-Hakim al-Naisaburi, "Taʾrikh Naisabur," facsimile ms contained in Richard N. Frye, ed., *The Histories of Nishapur* (Cambridge, MA: Harvard University Press, 1965). Qazvin—ʿAbd al-Rahim al-Qazvini, *Al-Tadwin fi akhbar Qazvin* (Beirut: Dar al-Kutub al-ʿIlmiya, 1987), 5 v. Gorgan—Hamza al-Sahmi, *Taʾrikh Jurjan aw kitab maʿrifa ʿulamaʾ ahl Jurjan* (Hyderabad: Osmania Oriental Publications Bureau, 1967). Baghdad—al-Khatib al-Baghdadi, *Taʾrikh Baghdad* (Beirut: Dar al-Kitab al-ʿArabi, [nd]), 14 v.

2. Sam Isaac Gellens, "Scholars and Travelers: The Social History of Early Muslim Egypt, 218–487/833–1094," unpublished doctoral dissertation, Columbia University, 1986, 70–1, 145.

3. Ambiguity haunts this ratio. In Arabic the words *Bazzaz* and *Bazzar* differ only by a dot above the final letter. *Bazzar* can mean a dealer in linseed oil. Or it can be a scribal error or misprint in the published edition of the *Taʾrikh Baghdad*. Since each of the first three volumes of this fourteen-volume compilation contain ten or more *Bazzars*, and the remaining volumes contain only a sprinkling, it appears as though the editors changed their minds about whether the absence of a dot signified a different trade or was just a scribal omission. The total of 258 given in table 2.1 lumps *Bazzaz* and *Bazzar* entries together. If they were separated, the ratio would be four to one instead of five to one.

4. A precise study of Jewish merchant activity based on letters preserved in the Cairo Geniza, a trove of manuscripts dating from the late ninth/third century onward, shows strong trading links between Egypt and Syria but very few between Syria and Iraq or Iran. Jessica Goldberg, "Geographies of Trade and Traders in the Mediterranean in the Eleventh Century: A Study Based on Documents from the Cairo Geniza," unpublished doctoral dissertation, Columbia University, 2006.

5. Mazzaoui, *The Italian Cotton Industry in the Later Middle Ages, 1100–1600* (Cambridge: Cambridge University Press, 1981), 17.

6. Robert Serjeant, *Islamic Textiles* (Beirut: Librairie du Liban, 1972).

7. Liu Xinru, *Silk and Religion: An Exploration of Material Life and the Thought of People, AD 600–1200* (Delhi: Oxford University Press, 1996), 156.

8. A. S. Tritton, *The Caliphs and Their Non-Muslim Subjects: A Critical Study of the Covenant of 'Umar* (London: H. Milford, Oxford University Press, 1930).

9. Mas'udi, *The Meadows of Gold*, cited in Liu, *Silk*, 135.

10. Abu Muhammad Ja'far b. Jarir al-Tabari, *The Reign of Mu'tasim (833–842)*, tr. Elma Marin (New Haven: American Oriental Society, 1951), 116.

11. The earliest known Islamic fabric is a specimen of Tunisian *tiraz* datable to the brief caliphate of Marwan I (684–85/64–65). However, it antedates the emergence of the contest between brocade and plain linen/cotton, and hence the *hadith* about fingers, because the silk embroidery is on a fabric with a typically complex brocade design. F. E. Day, "The Tiraz Silk of Marwan" in G. C. Miles, ed., *Archaeologica Orientalia in Memoriam Ernst Herzfeld* (Locust Valley, NY: J. J. Augustin, 1952), 39–61 and Plate VI.

12. Liu, *Silk*, 141–49. Mazzaoui presents a more realistic appraisal of *tiraz* in the context of cotton production in *Italian Cotton Industry*, 21–22.

13. For scores of examples including translations of inscriptions see 'Abd Allah Quchani, *Katibah'ha-yi sufal-i Nishabur* (Tehran: Muzah-i Riza 'Abbasi, 1986).

14. Esin Atil, *Freer Gallery of Art Fiftieth Anniversary Exhibition*, vol. 3, *Ceramics from the World of Islam* (Washington, DC: Smithsonian Institution, 1973), 26–29.

15. Charles K. Wilkinson, *Nishapur: Pottery of the Early Islamic Period* (New York: The Metropolitan Museum of Art, [nd]), 3–7.

16. Richard W. Bulliet, "Pottery Styles and Social Status in Medieval Khurasan," in A. Bernard Knapp, ed., *Archaeology,* Annales*, and Ethnohistory*, 74–82

17. The cotton revolution did eventually affect Zoroastrian practice. "In modern times, bodies are washed with water for purification, then dressed in white garments and wrapped in a white cotton shroud and buried." (Personal communication from Jamsheed K. Choksy.) More generally on Zoroastrian funerary practice see Jamsheed K. Choksy, "Aging, Death, and the Afterlife in Zoroastrianism," in *How Different Religions View Death and Afterlife*, 2nd ed., C. J. Johnson and M. G. McGee, eds. (Philadelphia: Charles Press, 1998), 246–263.

18. The exact meaning of *karbas* in the early Islamic centuries is uncertain, but one specialist on Iranian textiles in the eighteenth century describes it this way: "[A] coarse white [cotton] cloth of loose texture and varying quality was made for home use in every village. It was used by the poor in many articles of clothing, and as garment linings by the middle class. . . . And it was used as a tent material. . . ." Willem Floor, "Economy and Society: Fibers, Fabrics, Factories," in *Woven from the Soul, Spun from the Heart: Textile Arts of Safavid and Qajar Iran 16th-19th Centuries,* Carol Bier, ed. (Washington, DC: The Textile Museum, 1987), 26.

19. Richard Eaton, *The Rise of Islam and the Bengal Frontier, 1204–1760* (Berkeley: University of California Press, rpt 1996).

20. Malcolm Gladwell, *The Tipping Point: How Little Things Can Make a Big Difference* (New York: Little, Brown and Company, 2000), ch. 5.

21. J. Behnam, "Population," in *The Cambridge History of Iran,* vol. 1 (Cambridge: Cambridge University Press, 1968), 479.

22. For regional differentials in rates of conversion, see Bulliet, *Conversion*, ch. 7–10.

23. Safinezhad, *Boneh*, 143–55 contains a specific discussion of how one *sahra'* functions in the Torbat-e Jam district of Khurasan.

24. Abu Nuʿaim, *Akhbar Isbahan*, vol. 1, 37. I am grateful to Hossein Kamaly for bringing this anecdote to my attention.

25. Cited and discussed in Étienne de la Vaissière, *Sogdian Traders: A History*, James Ward, tr. (Leiden: Brill, 2005), 239. The use of *karbas* to designate fine cloth in this passage differs from other usages in which it is a coarse cloth.

## CHAPTER 3.  THE BIG CHILL

1. Carter Vaughn Findley, *The Turks in World History* (Oxford: Oxford University Press, 2005), 15.

2. Ibn al-Jawzi, *Al-Muntazam fi Ta'rikh al-Muluk wa'l-Umam* (Heydarabad: Matbaʿat Daʾirat al-Maʿarif al-ʿUthmaniyah, 1357–59 [1938–40]), vol. 6, 201–202.

3. Ibid., vol. 7, 237.

4. Ibid., vol. 6, 156.

5. Ibid., vol. 6, 39.

6. David Koenig, "Medieval Winters in Baghdad: A Study in the History of Climate Between 296 A.H. and 493 A.H. Based on Ibn al-Jawzi's *Kitab al-Muntazam*," unpublished MA thesis, Columbia University, 1991.

7. R. D'Arrigo, G. Jacoby, et al. "1738 Years of Mongolian Temperature Variability Inferred from a Tree-Ring Record of Siberian Pine," *Geophysical Research Letters*, 28 (2001), 543–46.

8. For a recent and detailed review of the evidence for and against a Medieval Warm Period and a Little Ice Age—primarily the latter—see Willie Soon and Sallie Baliunas, "Reconstructing Climatic and Environmental Changes of the Past 1000 Years: A Reappraisal," *Energy & Environment* 14:2–3 (March 2003): 233–39.

9. Because the climate of China is affected by the global monsoon system, which does not influence the northern Middle East, the relevance of temperature fluctuations there to weather patterns in the northern Middle East is unclear. Nevertheless, it seems reasonable to surmise that northern China at least would have been affected by any marked change in the intensity of the Siberian High. Unfortunately, the data available to nonspecialists pertain to China as a whole, and in a separate series to eastern China, but not specifically to northern China. The data covering China as a whole indicate no noteworthy cooling before the year 1090/482. At that point, however, temperatures did plummet

rapidly. Though the onset of this cold period is substantially later than what is indicated for Iran, it lasted in both areas until approximately 1130/524. (Yang Bao et al., "General characteristics of temperature variation in China during the last two millennia," *Geophysical Research Letters*, 10.1029/2001GL014485 [11 May 2002], available on-line at www.ncdc.noaa.gov/paleo/pubs/tan2003/tan2003.html.) This post-1090/482 episode of generally colder weather took place during a period of generally quite warm summers in northern China (Beijing), and thus may be presumed to relate specifically to cold winters. (Ming Tan et al., "Cyclic Rapid Warming on Centennial-Scale Revealed by a 2650-Year Stalagmite Secord of Warm Season Temperature," *Geophysical Research Letters* 30, no. 12, 1617 (June 2003), available on-line at *www.ncdc.noaa.gov/paleo/pubs/ tan2003/tan2003.html*) I am grateful to Professor Victor B. Lieberman for his cautionary thoughts about climate effects in China.

10. For a classic introduction to climate history see Emmanuel Le Roy Ladurie, *Times of Feast, Times of Famine: A History of Climate since the Year 1000*, tr. Barbara Bray (Garden City, NY: Doubleday, 1971).

11. "Was there a 'Little Ice Age' and a 'Medieval Warm Period'?" in 2001 report of the Intergovernmental Panel on Climate Change: *www.grida.no/climate/ipcc_tar/wg1/070 .htm*

12. Willie Soon, "Reconstructing," 270.

13. G. C. Jacoby, R. D. D'Arrigo, et al., "Mongolian Tree Rings and 20th-Century Warming," *Science* 273, no. 5276 (1996): 771–73.

14. Iran was stricken in 1870–72/1286–88, Russia and the Ottoman Empire in 1873–74/1289–90. The severe famine in northern China in 1876–79/1292–95 may be related to these catastrophes.

15. For example, both Mongolian data series show a near-record cold snap at the outset of the seventeenth/second decade of the eleventh century. Historical narratives of the time report severe famine stalking Russia from 1602/1010 to 1604/1012 during the last years of the reign of Tsar Boris Godunov, and catastrophic famine striking Ottoman Anatolia and touching off a "Great Flight," or Büyük Kaçgun, that saw thousands of peasants abandoning their barren villages. In this case, however, the cold was truly global and was caused by the eruption on February 19, 1600, of the Huaynaputina volcano in Peru. I wish to thank Professor Sam White for alerting me to this correlation.

16. Hamza b. al-Hasan al-Isfahani, *Kitab ta'rikh sanni muluk al-ard wa'l-anbiya* (Berlin: Buchdruckerei und Verlagsanstalt "Kaviani," [nd]), 122. I wish to thank Dr. Asef Kholdani for bringing this to my attention.

17. For a sample of such a study of nearby Turkey, see Peter Ian Kuniholm, "Archaeological Evidence and Non-evidence for Climatic Change," in S. K. Runcorn and J.-C. Pecker, eds., *The Earth's Climate and Variability of the Sun Over Recent Millennia* (London: The Royal Society, 1990), 645–55.

18. Ibn al-Jawzi, *Al-Muntazam*, vol. 8, 25.

19. Ibid., 28.

20. Ibid., 36.

21. Ahmad ibn Fadlan, *Risalat Ibn Fadlan fi wasf al-rihla ila bilad al-Turk wa'l-Khazar wa'l-Rus wa'l-Saqaliba* (Damascus: Matbu'at al-Majma' al-'Ilmi al-'Arabi, 1959/1379). I wish to thank Prof. Karen Pinto for bringing the relevant passages from this text to my attention, and her mother Adele Pinto, for making her English version of a Russian translation of the work available to me.

22. Ibid., 83.

23. Ibid., 84–85.

24. Ibid., 86–90.

25. Al-Isfahani, *Kitab Sanni*, 124.

26. Ibid.

27. Abul'l-Fazl Beyhaqi, *The History of Beyhaqi,* tr. with commentary by C. E. Bosworth and revised by M. Ashtiany, Persian Heritage Series, 3 vols. (New York: 2009).

28. Wilhelm Barthold , *Turkestan Down to the Mongol Invasion*, 3e (London: Luzac & Co., 1968), 298, n. 4.

29. Beyhaqi vol. 2, 209.

30. Beyhaqi, vol. 2, 247–48.

31. Beyhaqi, vol. 2, 299.

32. Beyhaqi, vol. 2, 304.

33. Ibid.

34. Abu al-Hasan 'Ali Bayhaqi "Ibn Funduq," *Tarikh-e Baihaq*, 2e (Tehran: Ketabforushi Foroughi, [nd]), 268, 273.

35. Abu Nasr Muhammad Al-Utbi, *Kitab-i-Yamini,* James Reynolds, tr. (London: Oriental Translation Fund, 1858), ch. 33. Full text of this chronicle is available at persian.pack-hum.org/persian/intro.html

36. Ibn al-Athir, *Al-Kamil fi'l-Ta'rikh,* vol. 10 (Beirut: Dar Sadir-Dar Beirut, 1966/1386), 291.

37. Ibid., 301.

38. Dorothea Krawulsky, ed. and tr., *Briefe und Reden des Abu Hamid Muhammad al-Gazzali* (Freiburg im Briesgau: Klaus Schwarz Verlag, 1971), 65. I am most grateful to Professor Kenneth Garden for this reference.

39. These points are discussed at length with corroborating evidence in Bulliet, *View from the Edge*, ch. 8–9.

40. Printed chintzes and calicos rather than plain cloth have been the hallmark of Iranian cotton production during the past three centuries. See *Woven from the Soul, Spun from the Heart*, 29, 146–50.

41. André Miquel, *La géographie humaine du monde musulman jusqu'au milieu du 11ᵉ siècle,* vol. 1 (Paris: Mouton, 1967–1988).

42. Hamd-Allah Mustawfi, *The Geographical Part of the* Nuzhat-al-Qulub, G. Le Strange, tr. (London: Luzac & Co., 1919).

43. Ruy Gonzalez de Clavijo, *Narrative of the Embassy of Ruy Gonzalez de Clavijo to the Court of Timour at Samarcand, A.D., 1403–6*, Clements R. Markham, tr. (London: Hakluyt Society, 1859).

44. Daniel Martin Varisco, *Medieval Agriculture and Islamic Science: The Almanac of a Yemeni Sultan* (Seattle: University of Washington Press, 1994), 202.

45. For an analysis of the depressive effect of low temperatures on the germination of winter wheat see Burhan Ozkan and Handan Akcaoz, "Impacts of Climate Factors on Yields for Selected Crops in Southern Turkey," *Mitigation and Adaptation Strategies for Global Change*, 7 (2002): 367–80. I am greateful to Professor Sam White for bringing this article to my attention.

46. Bulliet, *View from the Edge*, ch. 8.

47. Two abbreviated manuscripts of this work are contained in Richard N. Frye, *Histories of Nishapur*.

48. Cf. table 1.1 and accompanying discussion in chapter 1.

49. Beyhaqi, vol. 1, 246–47.

50. 'Abd al-Karim al-Sam'ani, *Adab al-imla' wa'l-istimla'* Max Weisweiler, tr. (Leiden: E.J. Brill, 1952), 30.

51. Bulliet, *Conversion*, ch. 5.

52. Beyhaqi, vol. 1, 162.

## CHAPTER 4. OF TURKS AND CAMELS

1. Wilhelm Barthold , *Turkestan Down to the Mongol Invasion*, 3e (London: Luzac & Co., 1968), 285.

2. Naseem Ahmad, *Religion and Politics in Central Asia Under the Saljuqs* (Srinagar: Sahil Publications, 2003), 49. The word *cattle* obviously follows the British usage, meaning hoofed livestock in general.

3. Ibid.

4. Carter Vaughn Findley, *The Turks in World History* (Oxford: Oxford University Press, 2005), 68

5. Anne K. S. Lambton, "Aspects of Saljuq-Ghuzz Settlement in Persia," in *Islamic Civilization, 950–1150*, D.H. Richards, ed. (Oxford: Cassirer, 1973), 111.

6. For a discussion of horse domestication see Richard W. Bulliet, *Hunters, Herders, and Hamburgers* (New York: Columbia University Press, 2005), ch. 5–7.

7. An extensive collection of photographs of this part of Iran that is currently occupied in part by Turkoman nomads is available on-line at: www.turkmensahra.com

8. Wilhelm Barthold, *An Historical Geography of Iran*, Svat Soucek, tr. (Princeton: Princeton University Press, 1984), 88.

9. Robert A. Lewis, "Early Irrigation in West Turkestan," *Annals of the Association of American Geographers*, 56/3 (September, 1966): 472.

10. Bayhaqi, vol. 2, 133.

11. Jean Aubin has shown that when true horse nomads traversed the area in Mongol and Timurid times they preferred east–west routes that followed the valley between the Binalud and Kopet Dagh. The comparatively flat east–west route that ran south of the Binalud had long been preferred by Silk Road caravaneers, with their enormous strings of camels. But it was too arid for the Mongol horse herds. The sources do not even mention the third alternative from Nasa to Abivard to Sarakhs. ("Réseau pastoral et réseau caravanier. Les grand'routes du Khurassan à l'époque mongole," *Hautes Études Islamiques et Orientales d'Histoire Comparée*, IV *Le Monde Iranien et l'Islam* [Paris: Librairie Minard, 1971], 105–30.)

12. Barthold, *Historical Geography*, 88.

13. *Hudud al-ʿAlam "The Regions of the World": A Persian Geography*, V. Minorsky, tr. (London: Luzac & Co., 1937), 104.

14. *Hudud al-ʿAlam*, 133–34.

15. Ibid.

16. Richard W. Bulliet, *The Camel and the Wheel* (Cambridge, MA: Harvard University Press, 1975).

17. The websites are *www.ansi.okstate.edu/breeds/other/camel/arvana/* and *www.turkmens.com/Turkmenistan.html*. The scientific source, which I have not been able to consult, is N. G. Dmitriev and L. K. Ernst, *Animal Genetic Resources of the USSR,* Food and Agriculture Organization Animal Production and Health Paper No. 65, 1985. In addition to this apparently scientific finding, a nineteenth-century European traveler to the city of Khiva in Khwarazm noted that "the dromedaries, both *nar* and *irkek* breeds, are sensitive to cold." ("Tartarie," in Louis Dubeux and V. Valmont, *Tartarie, Beloutchistan, Boutan et Népal* [Paris: Didot Frères, 1848], 62.) In modern Turkmen usage, the word *nar* means the same thing as *bukht*, a hybrid. *Irkek*, however, should denote a two-humped camel, not a dromedary (one-humped camel). Regardless of this terminological confusion, however, the report confirms the susceptibility of camels to cold.

18. ʿAmr b. Bahr al-Jahiz, *Kitab al-Hayawan* (Beirut: Dar Ihyaʾ al-Turath al-ʿArabi, [nd]), vol. 7, 135.

19. Ibid., vol. 3, 434. I mistranslated this passage in *The Camel and the Wheel.*

20. Ahmad ibn Fadlan, *Risalat Ibn Fadlan fi wasf al-rihla ila bilad al-Turk waʾl-Khazar waʾl-Rus waʾl-Saqaliba* (Damascus: Matbuʿat al-Majmaʿ al-ʿIlmi al-ʿArabi, 1959/1379), 83.

21. "Court Art of Sogdian Samarqand in the 7th century AD: Some remarks to an old problem," A web publication by Markus Mode, 2002 (www.orientarch.uni-halle.de/ ca/afras/index.htm).

22. A. Gubaev, "Raskopki Zamka Ak-depe," in B. A. Rybakov, *Arkheologischeskie Otkrytiya 1971 goda* (Moscow, 1972),536–37.

23. *The Cambridge History of Iran*, vol. 3(1) (Cambridge: Cambridge University Press, 1983), 254–55, pl. 24:14–15.

24. Ahmad al-Yaʿqubi, *Kitab al-Buldan*, de Goeje, ed. (Leiden: E.J. Brill, 1892), 277.

25. The cross-breeding of camels and the relevant sources are extensively discussed in Bulliet, *Camel*, chap. 6. The Arabic column in the accompanying table of definitions is incomplete on the meaning of *bukht*.

26. Al-Jahiz, vol. 1, 138.

27. Bulliet, *Camel*, 144–45.

28. Ibn Fadlan, *Risalat*, 86.

29. Ibn Hawqal, *Configuration*, 436. The translators mistakenly render *bukht* as "Bactrian," but the context makes the proper identification clear.

30. *Hudud al-ʿAlam*, 108.

31. Bayhaqi, vol. 2, 95.

32. Bayhaqi, vol. 2, 133.

33. Bayhaqi, vol. 2, 131.

34. Bayhaqi, vol. 2, 396.

35. Ibn Hawqal, *Configuration*, 413.

36. Professor Karen Pinto has greatly informed my understanding of Islamic cartographic issues, especially regarding the placement of the Oghuz.

37. Among important recent works see Jürgen Paul, *Herrscher, Gemeinwesen, Vermittler: Ostiran und Transoxanien in vormongolischer Zeit* (Beirut: Franz Steiner Verlag Stuttgart, 1996); and Omid Safi, *The Politics of Knowledge in Premodern Islam: Negotiating Ideology and Religious Inquiry* (Chapel Hill: University of North Carolina Press, 2006).

38. Table 4.1 was compiled from Abu al-Fath ʿAbd al-Hayy Ibn al-ʿImad, *Shadharat al-dhahab fi akhbar man dhahab*, 8 v. (Cairo: Maktaba al-Qudsi, 1931–32). The work used to test the reliability of the findings was Abu ʿAbd Allah Muhammad al-Dhahabi, *Kitab al-ʿibar fi khabar man ghabar*, ed. Salah al-Din Munajjid and Fuʾad Sayyid, 5 vols. (Kuwait: Office of Printing and Publication, 1960–66). For further discussion see Bulliet, *Conversion*, ch. 2.

39. Bulliet, *Patricians*, ch. 5–6; Bulliet, *View from the Edge*, ch. 8–9.

40. Bulliet, *Patricians*, Part II; Bulliet, *View from the Edge*, ch. 9.

41. A. Kazhdan and Ann Wharton Epstein, *Change in Byzantine Culture in the Eleventh and Twelfth Centuries* (Berkeley: University of California Press, 1985), 26. The authors express some reservations about the accuracy of this general view, but the evidence they cite to the contrary comes from Greece and Macedonia rather than from eastern Anatolia, where the impact of the Siberian High would have been most strongly felt.

42. Famines affected Kievan Russia in 1024/394, 1071/463, and 1092/484. How these may have correlated with weather events in Iran remains to be researched. Janet Martin, *Medieval Russia 980–1584* (Cambridge: Cambridge University Press, 1995), 60.

43. See, for example, Safi, *Politics of Knowledge*, ch. 2.

44. Discussions of what numismatists call the "silver famine" concentrate on the disappearance of silver coins in the eleventh/fifth century, but the debasing of silver dirhams in

the tenth/fourth century was remarked on at the time. Ibn Fadlan in 921/308 comments disparagingly on the adulteration of dirhams in Bukhara and Khwarazm. (*Risalat*, 79, 82).

45. George C. Miles, *The Numismatic History of Rayy* (New York: The American Numismatic Society, 1938). Miles added many specimens to this corpus before his death in 1975, but a second edition of his book has never been published. Nevertheless, it is unlikely that the added coins substantially alter the ratios of gold and silver.

46. Lambton, "Aspects," discusses at length the wider migrations of the Oghuz in Iran.

47. Bulliet, *Camel*, 231–34.

### CHAPTER 5. A MOMENT IN WORLD HISTORY

1. Richard N. Frye, *The Golden Age of Persia: The Arabs in the East* (London: Weidenfeld and Nicholson, 1975).

2. The most complete coverage, dynasty by dynasty, is in Richard N. Frye, ed., *The Cambridge History of Iran*, vol. 4, *From the Arab Invasion to the Saljuqs* (Cambridge: Cambridge University Press, 1975).

3. For recent one-volume examples see Elton Daniel, *The History of Iran* (Westport: The Greenwood Press, 2000); Gene R. Garthwaite, *The Persians* (Hoboken, NJ: Wiley-Blackwell, 2005); and Michael Axworthy, *A History of Iran: Empire of the Mind* (New York: Basic Books, 2008).

4. Hamza al-Sahmi, *Ta'rikh Jurjan aw kitab ma'rifa 'ulama' ahl Jurjan* (Hyderabad: Osmania Oriental Publications Bureau, 1967), 134–35.

5. Richard W. Bulliet, *Islam: The View from the Edge* (New York: Columbia University Press, 1994), 136–37.

6. Anne K. S. Lambton, "Aspects of Saljuq-Ghuzz Settlement in Persia," in *Islamic Civilization, 950–1150*, D. H. Richards, ed. (Oxford: Cassirer, 1973), 116.

# Index

Abbasid caliphate, 119, 127, 136; aesthetics of, 51, 53, 56; coins of, 122; eastern orientation of, 137–38

Abivard, 98, 103, 105

Achaemenid empire, 24, 128

*Adab al-imlaᶜ waˀl-istimlaᶜ* (al-Samᶜani), 91

aesthetics, dueling, 52, 56, 58–59

Afghanistan, 6, 10, 87, 99, 106, 122, 130

al-Afshin, 53

agriculture: and climate change, 69, 84, 85–86, 120, 135, 136, 140–41; cotton *vs.* grain in, 16, 30, 34–38, 46, 131, 132, 134; in history, 144; in Iraq, 44–45; and Islam, 59, 60–62, 65; in pre-Islamic Iran, 129; Sasanid, 12–13, 34; Seljuq, 121, 135–36; summer crops in, 16, 22, 38, 42, 64, 65, 87–88, 131; taxation of, 121, 122, 123; and trade, 15–16. *See also* cotton; grain

Algeria, 138

Ali, caliph, 49

Anas, Malik b., 50

Anatolia, 137, 152n15; camels in, 107, 108, 126; climate change in, 69, 76, 84, 120; migration to, 135, 136; Oghuz in, 121, 135; Persian language in, 141–42; and Siberian High, 73, 156n41

Arab conquest, viii, 1, 14; and camels, 108, 123–24; and conversion, x, 31, 60; and cotton production, 43, 64; and culture, 51, 59, 131; and land ownership, 15–16; and language, 8, 128, 139–42; and trade, 49, 129–30; and urbanization, 15, 46

Arab culture, 52, 56, 58–59

Arabic language, 8, 56; *fulanabad* names in, 30, 34, 41, 59; literature in, 127, 140–41; *vs.* Persian language, 128, 139–42; place-names in, 33–34, 62

Arabic script, 132, 140, 141; on pottery, 56–57, 68, 91–92; on *tiraz* fabric, 54–56, 92–94

Arabs: camels of, 112–13; clothing of, 54, 64–65, 68, 91, 131–32, 133; and cotton, 60; in Iran, 28, 40–41, 52–54, 56, 127, 130–31; names of, 30–33. *See also* Muslims

Armenia, 120–21

Ashraf, Ahmad, 21, 22

Ashtor, Eliyahu, viii

Australia, 9

Bactria, 7, 102

Baghdad, 3, 41, 127, 128, 141; cold weather in, 69, 70–73, 75, 77–78; and cotton,

Baghdad (*continued*)
    44–46, 54, 137; eastern orientation of,
    137–38; modern weather in, 71; and silk,
    54, 132
Bahram Gur, Shah, 124, 125, 126
Baker, Patricia L., 6
Baliunas, Sallie, 75
Balkh, 108, 109, 112, 130
Barthold, Wilhelm, 81, 97, 102, 104
Basra, 45
Bayhaqi, Abu al-Fazl, 79–81, 83, 90, 103,
    104, 113–17
*bazzaz* (dealer in cotton cloth), 44–45, 54, 89
Bengal, east, 60–61
Big Chill, 69–95; and cotton, 11, 66, 69, 72,
    86–95, 96; and Islam, 118–19, 141–43;
    Mongolian tree-ring evidence for, 2,
    72–73, 74, 76, 77, 84, 85, 86, 117;
    recovery from, 95, 124, 136; and Siberian
    High, 73–74, 76–78, 87, 93, 120,
    156n41; and social unrest, 85–86,
    120–21, 134. *See also* climate change
biographical dictionaries (*tabaqat*), 2–4, 32;
    occupational names in, 43–44; Sunnis
    *vs.* Shi'ites in, 142–43
*boneh* (work team) system, 25–26, 27, 65;
    alternate terms for, 62–63
Braudel, Fernand, 143
Buddhism, 7
Bukhara, 101, 122; and camels, 111, 113; and
    cotton, 8, 16, 42, 66–67, 86; Oghuz in,
    114, 116
al-Bukhari, 47–49
burial customs, 51, 60, 68
Buyid dynasty, 122, 141
Byzantine empire, 9

Caetani, Leone, viii
camel herders (*sarbanan*), 102–3, 105–6,
    111–14, 121, 134

camels, 10–11, 100, 144, 155n11; Arvana
    breed of, 107, 108; and climate, 79, 96,
    97, 106–7, 117; hybrid, 110–13, 117, 125,
    126, 135; images of, 123–26; in Iran,
    105–6, 123–24; for military, 96, 108, 111,
    113, 125, 134; and Oghuz, 105, 105–6,
    112–13, 134; one- *vs.* two-humped, 96,
    106–9, 117, 125; and trade, 96, 108,
    110–13, 121–22, 134–35; Turkoman
    breed of, 108, 112, 124
Carlyle, Thomas, ix
Central Asia, 99; camels in, 105–7; climate
    change in, 69, 120; and cotton, 7, 8, 11,
    16, 40, 42, 60, 131, 136; irrigation in, 16,
    40; migration from, 97–102, 103–4,
    134; Sunnis in, 122, 143; trade with, 5,
    13, 66, 122, 129
Chaghri (Seljuq chieftain), 98, 100, 103,
    105
China, 52, 111, 121, 136, 152n14; and climate
    change, 69, 85, 151n9; silk from, 9, 13, 93;
    trade with, 6–7, 13, 59, 129
Christians, 15, 31, 52, 60, 92, 127; Nestorian,
    99, 113
circumcision, 53
climate change, 2, 67, 69–95; and
    agriculture, 69, 84, 85–86, 120, 135, 136,
    141; and camels, 79, 96, 97, 106–7, 117;
    in Europe, 73–76; and factionalism,
    120, 134, 136; and famine, 37, 76, 81–84,
    134; as historical determinant, vii–x, 69,
    97; in Iran, 1, 69, 76, 84; and Isma'ili
    movement, 142–43; and language, 7–8,
    38, 140; and *longue durée*, 144; and
    Mediterranean region, 138; and
    migration, 86, 96, 97, 106, 135, 141–42.
    *See also* Big Chill
clothing: Arabic, 54, 64–65, 68, 91, 131–32,
    133; colors of, 50, 51, 65, 91; cotton,
    64–65, 67–68; dual aesthetics in,

irrigation, 12, 108; in Central Asia, 16, 40;
conversion to, 36–38; of cotton, 8, 22,
38, 40, 64, 102; of grain, 16, 22, 64, 131;
in history, 144; and land ownership,
15–16; and taxes, 38–39; types of, 42. See
also *qanats*
Isfahan, 8, 66, 80; cotton in, 42, 44, 86
al-Isfahani, Hamza, 77, 79, 80
Islam: and agricultural development,
60–62, 65; and climate change, 118–19,
141–43; and cotton, 8, 42–68, 119,
131–32, 137; factionalism in, 86, 118, 120,
133, 134, 136, 143, 144; and *fulanabad*
village names, 61–62, 63; in Iran,
127–28, 136; and land ownership, 15–16,
24, 60–61, 64, 130; language of, 139–41;
Shiʿites *vs.* Sunnis in, 122, 142–43; and
silk, 46, 47–54, 59–60, 91, 131;
sumptuary laws in, 50–54; and
urbanization, 8, 134. *See also* conversion
to Islam; elite, religious
*Islam: The View from the Edge* (Bulliet), 37
*Islamic Textiles* (Baker), 6
al-Ismaʿili, Abu Saʿd, 133
Ismaʿili movement, 138, 142

al-Jahiz, ʿAmr b. Bahr, 107, 108
al-Jawzi, Ibn, 71, 75, 76, 77–78, 79, 85
Jews, 15, 31, 52, 60, 127; Khazar, 99, 100, 113

*al-Kamil fiʾl-Taʾrikh* (Ibn al-Athir), 84
al-Karaji, 148n31
Karakum Desert, 101, 102, 102, 130; camels
in, 105–6, 107–8, 111, 135; migration
across, 103–4, 106; and Oghuz, 104, 113,
116; raids across, 104–6
*karbas* (cotton canvas), 7–8, 60, 67, 68, 88,
89, 91, 150n18
Kazakhstan, 99
Khotan, 7

Khurasan, 8, 44, 105, 113, 122; camels in, 108,
112, 125; cold weather in, 77, 84; cotton
in, 5, 42, 87; famine in, 82, 83–84; land
development in, 21, 63; Oghuz
migration to, 89, 102–3, 114, 115, 125,
134, 135; place-names in, 62–63; Seljuqs
in, 97–98, 99–100, 116, 117, 135;
urbanization in, 66, 134
Khusraw, Amir, 141
Khwarazm, 79–80, 102, 135; camels in, 107,
108, 109, 111, 112; Oghuz in, 104–5,
114–15, 116; and Silk Road, 116
Khwarazmshahs, 136
Khwarazmian period, 117, 118, 119
*Kitab al-Buldan* (Book of Lands;
al-Yaʿqubi), 109–10
*Kitab al-Hayawan* (Book of Animals;
al-Jahiz), 107
*Kitab al-Siyaq li Taʾrikh Naisabur*
(al-Farisi), 88
*Kitab-i Yamini* (al-ʿUtbi), 83
Kizilkum Desert, 101, 102
Kufa, 45
Kushan dynasty, 6, 7

Lambton, A.K.S., 27, 39, 100, 135
land ownership: and cotton, 16, 40;
investment in, 24–25; and Islamic law,
15–16, 24, 60–61, 64, 130; Muslim, 15–16,
30, 32–34, 38, 40, 62–63; and *qanats*, 30,
32–34; in Qom, 130–31; rural, 15–16, 25,
63, 67–68, 92, 129, 133; and Seljuq land
policies, 135–36; by *ulama*, 132, 133; and
urbanization, 139–40; and village
founding, 19, 24, 27, 38
language: and Arab conquest, 8, 128, 139–42;
and climate change, 7–8, 38, 140; and
cotton, 140–41, 146n16; and
place-names, 21–22. *See also* Arabic
language; Persian language

leather goods, 3, 88, 90, 93
linen, 3, 11, 13; Egyptian, 45, 50, 51, 55
Little Ice Age, 74–76
Liu, Xinru, 52, 56
*longue durée*, 144

madrasas, 143
Mahmud, Sultan of Ghazna, 97–98, 103,
    104, 105, 126; coins of, 122–23; and
    Oghuz, 113, 114, 135
Mamluks, Egyptian, viii
Manchus, 52
Manzikert, Battle of, 121
Marv, 6, 57, 66, 102, 130; camels in, 108, 109,
    111, 112; cotton in, 8, 16, 42, 86
Mas'ud, Sultan, 103, 113–14, 116, 135
Mazaheri, Aly, 21
*mazra'eh* (cultivated field), 33–34
Mazzaoui, Maureen Fennell, 49
Mecca, 45
Medieval Warm Period, 73–76
Medina, 45
Mediterranean region, 1, 138–39
Mesopotamia: and camels, 108, 126;
    climate change in, 69, 73, 76, 84; and
    Iran, 101, 128, 129, 136–37; urbanization
    in, 13
migration: and camels, 112–13; from Central
    Asia, 97–102, 103–4, 134; and climate
    change, 86, 96, 97, 105, 135, 142; of
    elite, 1–2, 86, 120, 136, 138, 140–41, 142,
    143, 144; across Karakum Desert,
    103–4, 105; and language, 140–41;
    Oghuz, 1, 69–70, 89, 96–126, 134–35;
    and pastoral nomadism, 89, 99–100;
    political causes of, 97–100; rural-urban,
    37, 87, 134; second Oghuz, 97, 102–3,
    104–5, 113–16, 135; southward, 100–102,
    103–4, 135; from Yemen, 28, 41, 64, 130,
    131

Miles, George C., 122
military, 67, 92, 100–101; camels for, 96, 108,
    111, 113, 125, 134; and Oghuz migration,
    98, 141–42, 144; Seljuq, 123, 135, 136
military garrisons, 15, 64, 109, 112
Miquel, André, 86
Mongolia, climate data from, 2, 72–78, 84,
    85, 86, 117
Mongol invasion, 17, 117–19, 121, 136, 140,
    142, 143
Morocco, 138
Morony, Michael, 31, 32
Mughal Empire, 60–61
Muhammad, ix, 24, 49, 50. See also *hadith*
*mulham* (cotton and silk textile), 56
*Al-Muntazam fi Ta'rikh al-Muluk
    wa'l-Umam* (al-Jawzi), 70
al-Muqtadir, Caliph, 79
Muslims, x, 42, 127, 140–41, 144; clothing
    of, 54, 64–65, 91, 92, 93; elite, 15–16, 25,
    52–54, 56, 58–59, 68, 130; land
    ownership by, 15–16, 30, 32–34, 38, 40,
    62–63; names of, 41, 43, 117–20, 138; vs.
    non-Muslims, 52–54; as religious
    scholars, 117–20, 142, 143; and silk, 46,
    47–54. See also elite, religious; Islam
Mustawfi, Hamd-Allah, 86
al-Mu'tasim, caliph, 53
*Al-Muwatta'* (*hadith* collection; Malik b.
    Anas), 50–51

names: Arab, 30–33; Biblical, 99, 113; and
    conversion to Islam, 32–33; Muslim, 41,
    43, 117–20, 138. See also *fulanabad*
    village names; place-names
names, occupational, 55, 122; and cotton, 59,
    65, 88–90, 93; of religious elite, 2–4, 40,
    43–44, 46–47, 93
Nasa, 98, 103, 105, 105, 115, 116
Newfoundland, 75